The best of a book
is not the thought
it contains,
but the thought
which it suggests.

~ O.W. Holmes

Given in memory of
J. William Henderson, Jr.
(Class of 1943)
and
Joey W. Henders

BLACK
AND
RIGHT

*The Bold New Voice of Black
Conservatives in America*

EDITED BY

*Stan Faryna
Brad Stetson
and
Joseph G. Conti*

PRAEGER

Westport, Connecticut
London

Library of Congress Cataloging-in-Publication Data

Black and right : the bold new voice of Black conservatives in America
  / edited by Stan Faryna, Brad Stetson, and Joseph G. Conti.
       p.   cm.
    Includes bibliographical references (p.   ) and index.
    ISBN 0–275–95342–4 (alk. paper)
    1. Afro-Americans—Politics and government.   2. Conservatism—
  United States.   I. Faryna, Stan, 1969–   .   II. Stetson, Brad.
  III. Conti, Joseph G.
  E185.615.B538   1997
  320.5'2'08996073—dc20   96–44674

British Library Cataloguing in Publication Data is available.

Library of Congress Catalog Card Number: 96–44674
ISBN: 0–275–95342–4

First published in 1997

Praeger Publishers, 88 Post Road West, Westport, CT 06881
An imprint of Greenwood Publishing Group, Inc.

Printed in the United States of America

The paper used in this book complies with the
Permanent Paper Standard issued by the National
Information Standards Organization (Z39.48–1984).

10 9 8 7 6 5 4 3 2 1

Copyright Acknowledgments

The editors and publisher gratefully acknowledge permission to reprint the following:

Clarence Thomas, "No Room at the Inn: The Loneliness of the Black Conservative." This chapter originally appeared in *Policy Review* no. 58 (10/01/91). Copyright © The Heritage Foundation. Reprinted by permission.

The chapter entitled "The Role of Black Conservative Leaders in the 1990s" is an edited transcript of a speech given by Representative Gary Franks at the Heritage Foundation on 2/7/91, Heritage Lecture #303. Reprinted by permission of the Heritage Foundation.

Selections from Saint Thomas Aquinas, *Summa Theologica*, translated by the Fathers of the English Dominican Province. Copyright © 1948 by Benzinger Brothers, Inc. Published by Christian Classics, 200 E. Bethany Dr., Allen, TX 75002.

For black conservatives across this nation,
in admiration of their courage and integrity.

CONTENTS

PREFACE

This is a book about—and for the most part by—black conservatives. For many years in this country, that phrase was considered an oxymoron. Conservatism was an ideology with a white face, and it was an intellectual impossibility that a black American might affirm it.

But that is rapidly changing. As this book will attest, social, political, religious, and economic conservatism is a point of view eagerly embraced and aggressively defended by many African Americans today.[1] They have journeyed through the pothole-ridden road of liberal promises and social reforms, and found that it ends in a frustrating dead end. They have returned to the family-centered traditions of earlier black Americans who knew that even under the economic deprivation and virulent racism of Jim Crow, the practice of diligence, thrift, self-reliance, and religious piety would enable one to succeed to as great a degree as one's social context would allow. For those black Americans, that degree was very limited. But for black Americans who are today moving into a new millennium—armed with the moral and legal victories of the civil rights movement, as well as a national conscience attuned to racial fairness—life presents no such immoral artificial barriers, despite a constant and now routinized claim to the contrary by what has become a hackneyed and self-serving civil rights establishment.

It is this positive conviction about the viability and equity of the American social and economic mainstream that most sharply distinguishes black conservatives from other black citizens. Yet, there is no single ideology called "black conservatism." Conservative African Americans speak in many different voices and hold a variety of sometimes divergent opinions and ideas, as this volume clearly shows. But they are all characterized by a sanguineness about the American prospect and a humanistic—as opposed to race-centered—consciousness that leads them to manifest social, political, and economic concerns that are not tinged with the hue of racial victimization which is so pervasive in the discourse of conventional black advocates.

In many ways this book presents the other side of the story told in an earlier book, *Challenging the Civil Rights Establishment: Profiles of a New Black Vanguard* (Joseph G. Conti and Brad Stetson, Praeger Publishers, 1993). That book focused on Thomas Sowell, Shelby Steele, Robert L. Woodson, and Glenn Loury, influential black conservative writers whose styles of analyses tend to be "academic" in nature.

Now, in *Black and Right*, mostly populist black conservatives speak in their own voices about issues important to them. This book tends to emphasize the grassroots aspect of black conservatism, and its reliance on common sense and common human experience. These essays are reflective and idiosyncratic, intending to show the special concerns of each contributor.

We became aware of many of these voices while one of the editors, Stan Faryna, was serving as director of Project 21, a black leadership organization. The boldness and clarity of the perspectives he heard expressed there made plain the need for a collection of articles illustrating the powerful, but underrecognized social critique of populist black conservatives. And so this book hopes to fill that void, providing a personal, social, and political portrait of black conservatives in America, in all their diversity and intellectual vigor.

The newness of the black conservative voice lies not in some nouveau quality to their ideas but rather in their burgeoning numbers and social influence. This will perhaps be one of the most politically significant trends in American public life as the century in which this country began to live out the true meaning of its creed—"All men are created equal"—comes to a close.

NOTE

1. A recent *Washington Post* poll found that 26 percent of black Americans identified themselves as conservatives, favoring smaller government, lower taxes, tougher crime laws, welfare reform, and an emphasis on personal initiative. For discussion

see Ralph Reiland, "Black Republicanism," *American Enterprise* (January/February 1996):8.

For a further register of black conservatives' concerns, see Glenn C. Loury and Shelby Steele, "A New Black Vanguard," *Wall Street Journal,* 29 February 1996, A16, and Gayle Pollard Terry, "Tony Brown: Black Empowerment—via a Computer," *Los Angeles Times,* 18 February 1996, M3.

For a discussion of the growing group of periodicals devoted to black conservative thought, see the op-ed essay by Jason L. Riley, "Black Conservatives Take to the Presses," *Wall Street Journal,* 17 July 1995.

ACKNOWLEDGMENTS

We would like to express our thanks to the Honorable Justice Clarence Thomas for allowing us to reprint his Fall 1991 *Policy Review* article, "No Room at the Inn: The Loneliness of the Black Conservative." The honesty and forcefulness of this article has made a profound impression on the minds of both black and white conservatives.

We would also like to thank Kristin Bramsen, Adam Meyerson, Cathy Mossett, and Richard Odermatt at the Heritage Foundation for helping us locate and granting permission to use material from *The Heritage Lectures* and *Policy Review*; the publications department of *The American Enterprise* magazine for assisting with our inquiries; and Lee Walker of the New Coalition for Economic and Social Change for his advice and guidance in pursuing this project.

Many thanks also to those who, though unable to participate in this project, were supportive of it: Stephan Brown, Clarence Carter, Jackie Cissell, Darlene Kennedy, Lance McCarthy, Hurley Green, August Scott, Stephen F. Smith, James Robinson, Elizabeth Wright, Bill Cleveland, Camille Harper, Raynard Jackson, Reverend Lester James, Sr., Star Parker, Alan Keyes, Armstrong Williams and Pastor Dwight Williams.

We also offer our heartfelt thanks to our contributors for all their great efforts, and to the kindest of friends who believed that this work was a worthy and noble enterprise: Bruce Leftwich, Reverend John Miller, and David Bovenizer. Our gratitude also to Margaret Moss and Matthew Cook for editorial assistance and layout—their heroic efforts will be long remembered; to our many friends and family through whose love and support we thrive; to Jae Shin Park, Don Rinella, and William and Louise Van Arsdale for their generosity, understanding, and undeserved kindnesses.

As well, deep gratitude is due The David Institute, Ken Ashford, Anthony Battaglia, Adele Conti, Mike Conti, Henry Clark, Donald E. Miller, Bradley Hawkins, Nina Stetson, Hannah and Sam Stetson, John and Carol Stetson, Dave and Doug Stetson, Anthony and Delia Trujillo, Frank Montejano, Steve Bivens, Steve Thacker, Arturo Silva, Anne D. Kiefer, Liz Murphy, Jim Dunton, and Desirée Bermani.

I

PERSPECTIVES ON
PERSONAL EXPERIENCE

The existential predicament of the black conservative in America is a profound one. On the one hand, when he expresses his sincerely held views, other black people often dismiss these positions as the disgusting cloying of an "Uncle Tom." On the other hand, white conservatives, unfamiliar with the realities of black life in America and the tremendous courage required for a black person to openly express conservative politics, underestimate the significance of his expression and so manifest a certain passivity and indifference to the black conservative's dilemma.

In this first section we hear from five black conservatives of vastly different backgrounds and prominence, all of them in their own way relating to the social and political frustrations they have personally experienced. In Chapter 1 Clarence Thomas recounts the isolation he felt in his years in Washington, D.C., preceding his nomination to the United States Supreme Court, an event that raised the profile of black conservatives considerably. Chapter 2 brings the reflections of Robert A. George, a West Indian native, on black identity and the experience of the black immigrant. Chapter 3 presents Kathleen M. Bravo's confrontation with a pervasive attitude held by those around her that because she is a black woman she must, quite naturally, hold certain opinions. In Chapter 4 Stuart DeVeaux recounts his experience with this kind of color-

coded thinking, and Chapter 5 features Lee Walker's developed perspective on the intellectual posture of the black conservative.

Together, these biographical moments yield a beginning look at the utterly unique and often challenging social context of black conservatives in America.

1

No Room at the Inn: The Loneliness of the Black Conservative

Clarence Thomas

There is some political and intellectual behavior in which you engage that keeps you from being a black person.

Roger Wilkins, professor

Much has been said about blacks and conservatism. Those on the Left smugly assume that blacks are monolithic and will by force of circumstances always huddle to the left of the political spectrum. The political Right watches this herd mentality in action, concedes that blacks are monolithic, picks up a few dissidents, and wistfully shrugs at the seemingly unbreakable hold of the liberal Left on black Americans. But even in the face of this, a few dissidents like Thomas Sowell and J. A. Parker stand steadfast, refusing to give in to the cult mentality and childish obedience that hypnotize black Americans into a mindless political trance. I admire them, and only wish I had a fraction of their courage and strength.

Many pundits have come along in recent years who claim an understanding of why so many blacks think right and vote left. They offer "the answer" to the problem of blacks failing to respond positively to conservatism. I for one am not certain there is such a thing as "the answer." And, even if there is, I assure you I do not have it.

I have only my experiences and modest observations to offer. First, I may be somewhat an oddity. I grew up under state-enforced segregation, which is as close to totalitarianism as I would like to get. My household, notwithstanding the myth fabricated by experts, was strong, stable, and conservative. In fact, it was far more conservative than many who fashion themselves conservatives today. God was central. School, discipline, hard work, and knowing right from wrong were of the highest priority. Crime, welfare, slothfulness, and alcohol were enemies. But these were not issues to be debated by keen intellectuals, bellowed about by rousing orators, or dissected by pollsters and researchers. They were a way of life; they marked the path of survival and the escape route from squalor.

MY GRANDPARENTS' FAMILY POLICY

Unlike today, we debated no one about our way of life—we lived it. I must add that my grandparents enforced the no debate rule. There were a number of concerns I wanted to express. In fact, I did on a number of occasions at a great price. But then, I have always found a way to get in my two cents.

Of course, I thought my grandparents were too rigid and their expectations were too high. I also thought they were mean at times. But one of their often-stated goals was to raise us so that we could "do for ourselves," so that we could stand on our "own two feet." This was not their social policy, it was their family policy—for their family, not those nameless families that politicians love to whine about. The most compassionate thing they did for us was to teach us to fend for ourselves and to do that in an openly hostile environment. In fact, the hostility made learning the lesson that much more urgent. It made the difference between freedom and incarceration; life and death; alcoholism and sobriety. The evidence of those who failed abounded, and casualties lay everywhere. But there were also many examples of success—all of whom, according to my grandfather, followed the straight and narrow path. I was raised to survive under the totalitarianism of segregation, not only without the active assistance of government but with its active opposition. We were raised to survive in spite of the dark oppressive cloud of governmentally sanctioned bigotry. Self-sufficiency and spiritual and emotional security were tools to carve out and secure freedom. Those who attempt to capture the daily counseling, oversight, common sense, and vision of my grandparents in a governmental program are engaging in sheer folly. Government cannot develop individual responsibility.

CONSERVATIVE GADGET IDEAS

I am of the view that black Americans will move inexorably and naturally toward conservatism when we stop discouraging them; when they are treated as a diverse group with differing interests; and when conservatives stand up for what they believe in rather than stand against blacks. This is not a prescription for success, but rather an assertion that black Americans know what they want, and it is not timidity and condescension. Nor do I believe gadget ideas such as enterprise zones are of any consequence when blacks who live in blighted areas know that crime, not lack of tax credits, is the problem. Blacks are not stupid. And no matter how good an idea or proposal is, no one is going to give up the comfort of the leftist status quo as long as they view conservatives as antagonistic to their interests, and conservatives do little or nothing to dispel the perception. If blacks hate or fear conservatives, nothing we say will be heard. Let me relate my experience as a designated black/conservative/Republican/Reagan appointee in the civil rights area—conservatism's soft underbelly as far as its opponents are concerned.

I begin by noting that there was much that many of us who were in the Reagan administration since the beginning could and should have done. This is at least as true for me as for anyone else. For example, I believe firmly that I should have taken a more aggressive stand against opponents of free enterprise and opponents of the values that are central to success in this society. For me, even more important, I should have been more aggressive in arguing my points with fellow members of the administration and with those who shared my political and ideological bent. With that said, let us take a look at my perception of the past few years.

In 1980 when Ronald Reagan was elected, I was a staffer for Senator John Danforth of Missouri. After the election, Thomas Sowell called to invite me to a conference in San Francisco, later named the "Fairmont Conference." It was his hope, and certainly mine, that this conference would be the beginning of an alternative group—an alternative to the consistently leftist thinking of the civil rights leadership and the general black leadership. To my knowledge, it was not intended that this group be an antagonist to anyone, but rather that it bring pluralism to the thinking and to the leadership of black Americans. As the conference at the Fairmont Hotel in San Francisco approached, there was much fanfare, considerable media coverage, and high hopes. In retrospect, however, the composition of the conference, the attendees, and their various motives for being there should have been an indication of the problems we would encounter in providing alternative thinking in our society.

Some of us went because we felt strongly that black Americans were being fed a steady diet of wrong ideas, wrong thinking, and certainly nothing approaching pluralism. There were some others, however, who appeared there solely to gain strategic political positions in the new Reagan administration. This would be the undoing of a great idea. But even so, hopes were high, expectations and spirits were high, and morale was high. For those of us who had wandered in the desert of political and ideological alienation, we had found a home, we had found each other. For me, this was also the beginning of public exposure that would change my life and raise my blood pressure and anxiety level. After returning from San Francisco, the *Washington Post* printed a major op-ed article about me and my views presented at the "Fairmont Conference." Essentially, the article listed my opposition to busing and affirmative action as well as my concerns about welfare. The resulting outcry was consistently negative.

CASTIGATED AND RIDICULED BY THE LEFT

Many black Republicans with whom I had enjoyed a working and amicable relationship on Capitol Hill were now distant, and some were even hostile. Letters to the editor castigated and ridiculed me. I was invited to a panel presentation by one organization, "Black Women's Agenda," and scolded by none other than Harold Washington of Chicago. Although I was initially shocked by the treatment I received, my spirits were not dampened. I was quite enthusiastic about the prospects of black Americans with different ideas receiving exposure. It was in this spirit that in 1981 I joined the Reagan administration as an assistant secretary in the Department of Education. I had, initially, declined taking the position of assistant secretary for civil rights simply because my career was not in civil rights and I had no intention of moving into this area. In fact, I was insulted by the initial contact about the position as well as my current position. But policies affecting black Americans had been an all-consuming interest of mine since the age of sixteen.

I always found it curious that, even though my background was in energy, taxation, and general corporate regulatory matters, I was not seriously sought after to move into one of those areas. But be that as it may, I was excited about the prospects of influencing change. The early enthusiasm was incredible. We had strategy meetings among blacks who were interested in approaching the problems of minorities in our society in a different way— among blacks who saw the mistakes of the past and who were willing to admit error and redirect their energies in a positive way. There was also considerable interest (among some white organizations) in black Americans who thought differently. But, by and large, it was an opportunity to be excited about the prospects of the future—to be excited about the possibilities of changing the course of history and altering the direction of social and civil rights policies in this country. Of course, for much of the media and for many organizations, we were mere curiosities. One person asked rhetorically, "Why do we need blacks thinking like whites?" I saw the prospects of proselytizing many young blacks who, like myself, had been disenchanted with the Left; disenchanted with the so-called black leaders; and discouraged by the inability to effect change or in any way influence the thinking of black leaders in the Democratic party.

THE BOB JONES FIASCO

But all good things must come to an end. During my first year in the Reagan administration, it was clear that the honeymoon was over. The emphasis in the area of civil rights and social policies was decidedly negative. In the civil rights arena, we began to argue consistently against affirmative action. We attacked welfare and the welfare mentality. These are positions with which I agree. But the emphasis was unnecessarily negative. It had been my hope, and it continues to be my hope, that we would expose principles and policies which by their sheer force would preempt welfare and race-conscious policies.

The winds were not taken out of our sails until early 1982 when we changed positions in the Supreme Court to support a tax exemption for Bob Jones University which had been previously challenged because of certain racial policies. Although the point being made in the argument that the administrative and regulatory arm of government should not make policies through regulations was valid, it was lost in the overall perception that the racial policies of Bob Jones University were being defended. In addition, the perception that the Reagan administration did not support an extension of the Voting Rights Act aggravated our problems.

I was intrigued by several events that surrounded both the *Bob Jones* decision and the handling of the Voting Rights Act. The decision to change positions in the *Bob Jones* case was made public on Friday afternoon simultaneously with the AT&T breakup. On the following Monday, I expressed grave concerns in a previously scheduled meeting that this would be the undoing of those of us in the administration who had hoped for an opportunity to expand the thinking of, and about, black Americans. A fellow member of the administration said rather glibly that, in two days, the furor over *Bob Jones* would end. I responded that we had sounded our death knell with that decision. Unfortunately, I was more right than he was.

With respect to the Voting Rights Act, I always found it intriguing that we consistently claimed credit for extending it. Indeed, President Reagan did sign it, and he did support the extension of the Voting Rights Act. But by failing to get out early and positively in front of the effort to extend the act, we allowed ourselves to be put in the position of opposing a version of the Voting Rights Act that was unacceptable, and hence we allowed the perception to be created that the Reagan administration opposed the Voting Rights Act, not simply a version of it.

INDIFFERENCE FROM THE RIGHT

Needless to say, the harangues to which we were subjected privately, publicly, and in all sorts of forums were considerable after these two policy decisions. There was no place that any of us who were identified as black conservatives, black Republicans, or black members of the Reagan administration could go without being virtually attacked and certainly challenged with respect to those two issues specifically and the Reagan administration generally. I remember a very good friend of mine complaining to me that he had been attacked simply for being my friend. Apparently the attack was so intense he simply left the event he was attending. They also made his date leave.

If that were not enough, there was the appearance within the conservative ranks that blacks were to be tolerated but not necessarily welcomed. There appeared to be a presumption, albeit refutable, that blacks could not be conservative. Interestingly, this was the flip side of the liberal assumption that we consistently challenged: that blacks were characteristically leftist in their thinking. As such, there was the constant pressure and apparent expectation that even blacks who were in the Reagan administration and considered conservative publicly had to prove themselves daily. Hence, in challenging either positions or the emphases on policy matters, one had to be careful not to go so far as to lose one's conservative credentials—or so it seemed. Certainly, pluralism on these issues was not encouraged or invited—especially from blacks. And if advice was given, it was often ignored. Dissent bore a price—one I gladly paid. Unfortunately, I would have to characterize the general attitude of conservatives toward black conservatives as indifference, with minor exceptions. It was made clear more than once that, since blacks did not vote right, they were owed nothing. This was exacerbated by the mood that the electoral mandate required a certain exclusivity of membership in the conservative ranks. That is, if you were not with us in 1976, do not bother to apply.

For blacks the litmus test was fairly clear. You must be against affirmative action and against welfare. And your opposition had to be adamant and constant, or you would be suspected of being a closet liberal. Again, this must be viewed in the context that the presumption was that no black could be a conservative.

CARICATURES AND SIDESHOWS

Needless to say, in this environment little or no effort was made to proselytize those blacks who were on the fence or who had not made up their minds about the conservative movement. In fact, it was already hard enough for those of us who were convinced and converted to survive. And our treatment certainly offered no encouragement to prospective converts. It often seemed that to be accepted within the conservative ranks and to be treated with some degree of acceptance, a black was required to become a caricature of sorts, providing sideshows of anti-black quips and attacks. But there was more—much more—to our concerns than merely attacking previous policies and so-called black leaders. The future, not the past, was to be influenced.

It is not surprising, with these attitudes, that there was a general refusal to listen to the opinions of black conservatives. In fact, it often appeared that our white counterparts actually hid from our advice. There was a general sense that we were being avoided and circumvented. It seemed that those of us who had been identified as black conservatives were in a rather odd position. This caused me to reflect on my college years.

The liberals, or more accurately, those on the Left, spent a great deal of time, energy, and effort recruiting and proselytizing blacks by playing on the ill treatment of black Americans in this country. They would devise all sorts of programs and protests in which we should participate. But having observed and having concluded that these programs and protests were not ours and that they were not in the best interest of black Americans, there was no place to go. There was no effort by conservatives to recruit the same black students. It seemed that those with whom we agreed ideologically were not interested and those with whom we did not agree ideologically persistently wooed us. I for one had the nagging suspicion that our black counterparts on the Left knew this all along, and just sat by and waited to see what we would do and how we would respond. They also knew that they could seal off our credibility with black Americans by misstating our views on civil rights and fanning the flames of fear among blacks.

ANIMOSITY FROM OTHER BLACKS

I failed to realize just how deep-seated the animosity of blacks toward black conservatives was. The dual labels of black Republicans and black conservatives drew rave reviews. Unfortunately the raving was at us, not for us. The reaction was negative, to be euphemistic, and generally hostile. Interestingly enough, however, our ideas themselves received very positive reactions, especially among the average working-class and middle-class black American who had no vested or proprietary interest in the social policies that had dominated the political scene for the past twenty years. In fact, I was often amazed with the degree of acceptance. But as soon as "Republican" or "conservative" was injected into the conversation, there was a complete about-face. The ideas were okay. The Republicans and conservatives, especially the black ones, were out.

Our black counterparts on the Left and in the Democratic party assured our alienation. Those of us who were identified as conservative were ignored at best. We were treated with disdain, regularly castigated, and mocked; and of course we could be accused of anything without recourse and with impunity. I find it intriguing that there has been a recent chorus of pleas by many of the same people who castigated us for open-mindedness toward those black Democrats who have been accused of illegalities or improprieties. This open-mindedness was certainly not available when it came to accusing and attacking black conservatives who merely had different ideas about what was good for black Americans and themselves.

RECKLESS MEDIA

The flames were further fanned by the media. I often felt that the media assumed that, to be black, one had to espouse leftist ideas and Democratic politics. Any black who deviated from the ideological litany of requisites was an oddity and was to be cut from the herd and attacked. Hence, any disagreement we had with black Democrats or those on the Left was exaggerated. Our character and motives were impugned and challenged by the same reporters who supposedly were writing objective stories. In fact, on numerous occasions, I have found myself debating and arguing with a reporter who had long since closed his notebook, put away his pen, and turned off his tape recorder.

I remember one instance when I first arrived at the Department of Education, a reporter, who happened to be white, came to my office and asked, "What are you all doing to cut back on civil rights enforcement?" I said, "Nothing! In fact, here is a list of all the things we are doing to enforce the law properly and not just play numbers games." He then asked, "You had a very rough life, didn't you?" To this, I responded that I did not; that I did indeed come from very modest circumstances but that I had lived the American dream; and that I was attempting to secure this dream for all Americans, especially those Americans of my race who had been left out of the American dream. Needless to say, he wrote nothing. I have not always been so fortunate.

There was indeed, in my view, a complicity and penchant on the part of the media to disseminate indiscriminately whatever negative news there was about black conservatives and to ignore or bury the positive news. It is ironic that six years ago, when we preached self-help, we were attacked ad infinitum. Now it is common among black Democrats to act as though they have suddenly discovered our historical roots and that self-help is an integral part of our roots. The media were also recklessly irresponsible in printing unsubstantiated allegations that portrayed us as anti-black and anti-civil rights.

Unfortunately, it must have been apparent to the black liberals and those on the Left that conservatives would not mount a positive (and I underscore positive) civil rights campaign. They were confident that our central civil rights concern would give them an easy victory since it was confined to affirmative action—that is, being against affirmative action. They were certain that we would not be champions of civil rights or would not project ourselves as champions of civil rights. Therefore, they had license to roam unfettered in this area claiming that we were against all that was good and just and holy, and that we were hell bent on returning blacks to slavery. They could smirk at us black conservatives because they felt we had no real political or economic support. And they would simply wait for us to self-destruct or disappear, bringing to an end the flirtation of blacks with conservatism.

Interestingly enough, I had been told within the first month of going to the Department of Education in 1981 that we would be attacked on civil rights and that we would not be allowed to succeed. It was as though there was a conspiracy between opposing ideologies to deny political and ideological choices to black Americans. For their part, the Left exacted the payment of a very high price for any black who decided to venture from the fold. And among conservatives, the message was that there is no room at the inn. And if there was, only under very strict conditions.

THE GOP'S FAILURE OF PRINCIPLE

It appears that we are welcomed by those who dangle the lure of the wrong approach and we are discouraged by those who, in my view, have the right approach. But conservatives must open the door and lay out the welcome mat if there is ever going to be a chance of attracting black Americans. There need be no ideological concessions, just a major attitudinal change. Conservatives must show that they care. By caring I do not mean the phony caring and tear-jerking compassion being bandied about today. I, for one, do not see how the government can be compassionate; only people can be compassionate and then only with their own money, their own property, or their own effort, not as that of others. Conservatives must understand that it is not enough just to be right. But why should conservatives care about the number of blacks in the Republican party? After all, it can be argued that the resources expended to attract black votes could be spent wooing other ethnic groups or other voters to vote Republican.

I believe the question of why black Americans should look toward conservative policies is best addressed as part of the general question, "Why should any American look toward conservative policies?" Conservatism's problem and the problem of the post-Reagan Republican party, the natural vehicle for conservatism, is making conservatism more attractive to Americans in general. In fact, our approach to blacks has been a paradigm of the Republican party as a whole. The failure to assert principles—to say what we are "for"—results in treating everyone as an interest group.

Blacks just happened to represent an interest group deemed not worth pursuing. Polls rather than principles appeared to control. We must offer a vision, not vexation. But any vision must impart more than a warm feeling that "everything is fine—keep thinking the same." We must start by articulating principles of government and standards of goodness. I suggest that we begin the search for standards and principles with the self-evident truths of the Declaration of Independence.

Now that even popular publications like *Time* magazine have decided to turn ethics into a cover story, there is at least some recognition that a connection exists between natural law standards and constitutional government. Abraham Lincoln made the connection between this and politics in his great pre–Civil War speeches. Lincoln talked not only about the immediate issue of slavery and its spread, but also about the whole concept of self-government—of men governing others by their consent, and of ruling oneself.

REEXAMINING NATURAL LAW

The need to reexamine natural law is patent. Yet it is more venerable than St. Thomas Aquinas. It both transcends and underlies time and place, race and custom. And, until recently, it has been an integral part of the American political tradition. Martin Luther King was the last prominent American political figure to appeal to it. But Lewis Lehrman's essay in *The American Spectator*[1] on the Declaration of Independence and the meaning of the right to life is a splendid example of applying natural law.

Briefly put, the thesis of natural law is that human nature provides the key to how men ought to live their lives. Without natural law, the entire American political tradition, from Washington to Lincoln, from Jefferson to Martin Luther King, would be unintelligible. According to our higher law tradition, men must acknowledge each other's freedom and govern only by the consent of others. All our political institutions presuppose this truth. Natural law of this form is indispensable to decent politics. It is the barrier against the "abolition of man" that C. S. Lewis warned about in his short modern classic.[2]

This approach allows us to reassert the primacy of the individual, and establishes our inherent equality as a God-given right. This inherent equality is the basis for aggressive enforcement of civil rights laws and equal employment opportunity laws designed to protect individual rights. Indeed, defending the individual under these laws should be the hallmark of conservatism rather than its Achilles' heel. And in no way should this be the issue of those who are antagonistic to individual rights and the proponents of a bigger, more intrusive government. Indeed, conservatives should be as adamant about freedom here at home as we are about freedom abroad. We should be at least as incensed about the totalitarianism of drug traffickers and criminals in poor neighborhoods as we were about totalitarianism in Eastern bloc countries. The primacy of individual rights demands that conservatives be the first to protect them.

RESPONSIBILITIES OF FREEDOM

But with the benefits of freedom come responsibilities. Conservatives should be no more timid about asserting the responsibilities of the individual than they should be about protecting individual rights.

The principled approach would, in my view, make it clear to blacks that conservatives are not hostile to their interests but aggressively supportive. This is particularly true to the extent that conservatives are now perceived as anti–civil rights. Unless it is clear that conservative principles protect all individuals, including blacks, there are no programs or arguments, no matter how brilliant, sensible, or logical, that will attract blacks to the conservative ranks. They may take the idea and run, but they will not stay and fraternize without a clear, principled message that they are welcome and well protected.

NOTES

This article originally appeared in the fall 1991 issue of *Policy Review*.
1. April 1987 issue.
2. C. S. Lewis, *The Abolition of Man* (New York: Macmillan, 1947).

2

NOTES OF A NONNATIVE SON: THE THIRD VISION

Robert A. George

Many immigrants come to America because they want to live an achieving, American-style life, leading to the paradox of immigrants preaching self-reliance to poorer, native-born Americans.

Lawrence Mead, political economist, *The New Politics of Poverty*

Who is the new black conservative? What is the road of the new black conservative? What is the path for African Americans as they seek a new life in the twenty-first century?

There is a wonderful scene in a recent HBO production, *The Tuskegee Airmen*, the story of the first black pilots in World War II. Two members of the squadron come out of nowhere to save a bomber under attack by a German squadron. The crew members of the bomber attempt to hail the black pilots, to no avail. "They must be on some separate frequency," says one of the white bombers. The irony cannot be lost on any thoughtful viewer.

Yes, the black pilots were on some separate frequency. The variable frequency—it hearkens back to W.E.B. Du Bois and his classic, *The Souls of Black Folk.* Du Bois recognizes a duality in the American black person. He writes of a twoness that black people feel. We are American, yet Negro—two souls, two thoughts, two unreconciled selves, always striving to be whole.

It is this same frequency hinted at by Ralph Ellison at the conclusion of *Invisible Man*, his seminal work of one man's search for identity and self-actualization amidst a world that does not understand him.

Both Du Bois and Ellison touch on the varied directions in which black Americans are torn as they strive to succeed. But the question before us—are there only two directions, two "frequencies," if you will—American and African? This writer believes that there is a third way, a third frequency, whose force will only get stronger as the twenty-first century comes into full force.

A Third Way

This is not precisely the same "Third Wave" that many (including Speaker of the U.S. House Newt Gingrich) discuss. That refers to the changes that the information age will have on our society. This third wave of which we are talking about here is the immigration wave. So far, it has been criticized and vilified, most stridently, interestingly enough, by many immigrants themselves. The immigrant third wave is of interest and also creates fear precisely because it stems from the so-called Third World: Asia, Africa, and the Caribbean. It should surprise no one that the most fervent immigration critics actually hail from not just the First World, but America's Old Country—Great Britain. These critics are Peter Brimelow, author of the acclaimed *Alien Nation*,[1] and John O'Sullivan, the editor of *National Review* magazine.

Race, however, is the ongoing tragic aspect of the American drama, affecting a wide range of everyday life, decisions both private and public. The most evil part of race happens when it explicitly comes together with politics. Decades after Jim Crow laws have been eliminated, we see the continuing effects of the nexus of race and politics in challenges going to the Supreme Court on various redistricting plans across the country, particularly in the South. At the heart of many of these situations is how African Americans are best able to choose who will represent them.

So many questions. Do I have answers? I can't say. I can only bear witness to my own journey, and frankly, even that is suspect. Do not believe those who attempt to be impartial witnesses of their own lives, for an autobiography is often a deception of the most artful sort. It can be so artful that even the writer does not completely understand the nature of his deceit. We always wish to put ourselves in the best light, cover up our flaws, elevate our achievements, or downplay our failures. This is merely human nature, transcending issues of race, class, or country of origin. Understanding this, I shall yet strive to be as honest as possible in this mini-memoir.

This is partly written on the night of my twenty-fifth anniversary of arriving in the United States of America. Born in Trinidad in 1962, followed by eight years in Great Britain, I came to the United States in 1971. Twenty-five years later, I ask myself. Who am I? Why am I here?

Coming to America, the child of a single mother, I stood in a country that was not my own and I tried to comprehend it. My birthplace was one island, and my foster home was another island—one that ruled the world for centuries. But since no man can be an island, I reached adulthood in my adoptive home, the dominant superpower of the twentieth century. Which country can I call a legitimate sire? Which country is willing to see me as legitimate? The truth is that I cannot separate myself from any of those "homes." Like many Americans I am a mutt—a mixture of diverse cultures and influences. This African-American man cannot live alone on an island of blackness.

This nation of immigrants places almost unfair demands on immigrants. It requires us, much as the departed souls in Greek myth did, to take a light bath in the river of forgetfulness and begin a new life. Parts of the old life remain. (I remember while first attending Catholic school in New York that my classmates teased me more for my then-strong British accent than for my color.) Yet, the immigrant is forced into absorbing American culture—which is far stronger than many would believe.

The 1990s immigrant understands the sense of duality as the African American. The 1990s immigrant is different from his Italian and Irish and Polish predecessor. He is a "person of color" as the Left would have us believe. The Caribbean person; the African person; the Mexican person; the Korean person—the immigrant is judged by where he is from (culturally as well as racially), yet he gains strength by knowing where he is from, just as he knows where he is and where he wants to be.

This immigrant third wave creates within the African-American newcomer a third eye. Yes, if one has lived in this country for any extended period, the Du Bois duality is present: "One American, one African." Yet, he is also consciously aware of the rhythms of life and the flow of change personally undergone. The resident African in America yearns for a visceral change that four hundred years seems not to have accomplished. The newcomer has a faith that some would call naive, but a faith nonetheless that change is possible, but it comes as much from within as without.

The naive faith stems from a peculiar sense of adventure. The newcomer recognizes that security is not guaranteed and sees opportunity in the vast American land. The immigrant hears the siren call of America and says to himself or herself: "I belong here as much as anyone." The question of legitimacy rarely enters the immigrant mind. He believes the song "This land is your land; this land is my land." The immigrant believes in the myth of America, long after America's black and white native sons have seemingly chosen to forget it.

The newcomer believes in adoption—adopting the whole country—"America," well before America adopts and accepts him. The immigrant revels in the diversity of the American experience. (As an illustrative aside, I was in a major East Coast department store recently, and I noticed three Asian women looking at clothes. They looked to be a teenager, her mother, and grandmother. They were speaking in their native language. What was so American about the situation was that the teenager appeared to be extolling the virtues of this overpriced clothing. The mother and grandmother found the clothing nice, but the arguments less convincing. There was a distinct tone that crossed language barriers.)

After four centuries of being thought of as illegitimate, can the African American tune into a different frequency—the frequency of the newcomer's third wave? He has been forced to see himself in two seemingly contradictory ways. Is there a third possibility? Is it too much to ask to begin to see with a third eye? Can we begin to see that we are more than either African or American? Can we see that we are more than just black? Can we see that we are the sum of many experiences?

Our experience is far greater than the "either/or" to be found in "choosing" between Martin or Malcolm. In the 1990s, our experience is encompassed in Colin Powell, Louis Farrakhan, Oprah Winfrey, businessmen such as Robert Johnson and Herman Cain, and millions of others. The challenge for the African American is to make the twenty-first century the century of re-immigration. We seek validity and legitimacy, not in the "motherland," but *this* land, which is our land. The manifest destiny of the African American is more American than it is anything else. We may have faced four centuries of rejection, but we do not have to accept a societal judgment of illegitimacy. The African American must adopt his own country. He must understand it intimately, recognize its faults, yet still master its culture and not succumb to it.

The African-American "third way" into the twenty-first century demands going beyond the false division between "segregation" or "integration." That is another either/or proposition that needlessly limits us. True, one message of the Million Man March was that personal responsibility and self-sufficiency mandate that the black community take greater control of its own affairs and resources. But we must realize that it is as impossible for us to thrive alone as it is for the United States to excel by cutting itself off from the possibilities of the global market. As the next century looms, African Americans will soon no longer be the "Number One" U.S. minority as Hispanics become a greater part of the general population. The traditional black/white metaphor will be done. Instead of castigating and rejecting our newest neighbors, bridges must be built between different minority communities.

What frequency is this writer on? His experience has created neither an irrational distrust of government nor a belief that racism no longer exists. Rather, it has forced him to recognize the truth that so much of life's successes and failures, regardless of race, have less to do with outside forces and more to do with family bonds (not amorphous "values"), personal choices, and internal balance. Those attributes serve to keep one anchored through the tempest-tossed seas of life. As those seeds are planted, they will nurture a person and a community prepared to take the journey to discover America and the excellence within her.

Look away from the lonely island, seek your destiny; it is right there above the horizon. Open your eyes—and take it.

NOTE

1. Peter Brimelow, *Alien Nation: Commonsense about America's Immigration Disaster* (New York: Random House, 1995).

3

"YOU LOOK LIKE A DEMOCRAT"

Kathleen M. Bravo

There's tremendous peer pressure among black people to not be a Republican.
Joshua Smith, political adviser

One day, while I was talking about politics with someone, she said to me, "You look like a Democrat." I have often wondered what that person meant. Did she say it just because I am black? Historically, African Americans have supported the Democratic party as they sought the aid of politicians. Promises of more jobs, social assistance programs, and other forms of aid were just the right remedy that minorities were seeking to relieve oppression. Instead, what we received was dependency on the federal government, decline in educational quality, and an increase in crime.

AN ODD MIX

Being a woman of color who is also politically conservative has had its challenges. I have had a difficult time being accepted by whites and, sadly enough, by African Americans as well. Both immediately assume that because of my color, I am in support of the "tax and spend" liberal, social assistance philosophy of the Democratic party. I was not surprised by the attitudes of the white community whose opinions and stereotypes have been dramatically influenced by the media's depiction of the black community. My shock and horror came when I realized that nonacceptance and criticism also came from the members of my own race.

Two people immediately come to mind: my cousin and my childhood friend. Black and college educated, both these women think that I am too conservative. My cousin, a registered nurse, questioned whether or not I knew what being a Republican meant. In retrospect, I doubt very seriously if she is at all familiar with the ideologies espoused by either the Democrat or Republican parties. I am sure, however, that she holds to the notion that the Republican party is made up solely of conservative, rich, white people.

My childhood friend was another story. She is neither politically active nor employed. She believes that whites are holding all blacks back. This is the same friend whom I helped to get a job in a large firm, only to find out that she turned down the job and has instead decided to remain on government assistance. Although she is physically capable of working, she prefers sitting at home and blaming others for her misfortunes.

A white co-worker of mine is a supporter of the Democratic party. She believes that the government should play an active and dominant role in prenatal, postnatal, and other child care programs. She blames me and my Republican party for a decline in government-subsidized financial aid for higher education. After I reminded her that working, as well as scholarships being provided by the private sector, could be other options for funding a college education, she grew silent. She suddenly remembered that her own daughter did, in fact, receive a scholarship from a major corporation in the area, which greatly helped to offset the expense of her college education.

GROUPTHINK

Unfortunately, my biggest disappointments usually do come from white conservatives who hold that "You Look Like a Democrat" attitude. The stereotype that my political position is a reflection of my race is wrong. As more African Americans reach middle and upper-middle-class status, we will continue to see a similar increase in the number of those people who espouse the conservative policies of the Republican party. It involves breaking away from that "group mentality" held by blacks and whites alike that says that an individual can only think, act, and live like those other members of his or her group and, therefore, be judged by that same standard. My greatest disappointment continues to lie in the fact that the whites' preconceptions of African Americans are, unfortunately, the same preconceptions that African Americans have grown to accept of themselves.

4

YOUNG, BLACK, AND REPUBLICAN

Stuart DeVeaux

Those [blacks] who oppose the usual civil rights methods regard the charge of racial betrayal—the charge that expressing opposing opinions serves whites not blacks— as an illegitimate insistence that only certain thought patterns and ideas are appropriate for those who are black.

Joseph G. Conti and Brad Stetson

It's a great surprise for most people when they meet me and I tell them that I am a Republican. They usually respond: "Oh really, why?" Then I go into my two- or three-minute speech on why I am a Republican: the values I hold to be true are reflected more in conservative thought than in that of the Left. Conservative insight into the responsibility of government and individuals led me to define myself as a Republican. The fact is, most blacks have a conservative understanding of people and things. They have a deep and abiding appreciation for traditional values. At the same time, though, they usually fail to recognize their conservative identity.

THE REAL BLACK IDENTITY

Although most people express surprise at the fact that I am a black Republican, the surprise turns to shock when I tell them that I am a graduate of Howard University—a school noted for its radical liberal character! They think it odd that my personal philosophy is incompatible with that of my alma mater. It is as if I was not expected to think for myself, but uncritically join in the groupthink going on at Howard University and other black schools.

But such groupthink is just race relations hype perpetrated by the media and the supposed spokespersons of the black community. This hype has gripped the dark imaginations of young adults who are searching for an identity that seems to be more mythic than real. In fact, the real black identity, a conservative one, which was lost in the moral confusion of the 1960s, was something to have held to tightly. The identity of the individual, however, will not be found in ideology. Individuals will discover who they are in the things they do and the reason for which they do them.

THE PROBLEM WITH DEMOCRATS

Black schools need to consider the failure of big government solutions among other failed liberal propositions. For example, the social problems that are destroying the black community (breakdown of the family, crime, education, lack of economic initiative, poverty, and welfare) grew out of thirty years of a well-meaning Democrat-controlled Congress. Despite these failures, Democrats have not given up their poor solutions. Although socialism proved a miserable failure, liberals want to keep the socialist spirit alive. Of course, those Democrats do not live with the consequences. They don't live in the inner cities. Their neighbors are not drug lords and trigger-happy gangsters.

Most likely, those Democrats have neighbors who are hard-working, church-going, and blue- and white-collar professionals. Of course, these Democrats also send their children to private schools and prepare them to meet the challenges in life with intelligence, creativity, and persistence. They don't teach their kids to feel sorry for themselves and collect welfare checks. I would be very surprised if they did. The point is that they live in a different world than the world in which their propositions fall like bombs. They can afford to be liberals.

Black Americans cannot afford to be liberals—not unless they are making millions of dollars in sports or the entertainment business. We cannot afford sexual revolutions and experiments in the family. We cannot afford throwing out the church. We cannot afford doing drugs. In fact, we are still paying the debt run up by these practices—a debt that is beyond the means of all the money government can throw at the social ills destroying the black community.

UP FROM SLAVERY

Again and again, liberals and the black leadership seem to want to prescribe the same failed government solutions. Obviously, black Americans need to ask for a "second opinion." It has become painfully clear that the solutions prescribed not only are band aids (at best), but also do more harm than good. Their programs and rhetoric have destroyed an authentic identity that had belonged to black Americans—an identity grounded in high moral standards and self-determination.

The character of this identity was such that it could make giants of men and statesmen of slaves—sometimes to the individual's own amazement. An example of this amazement at one's own ability to persevere against the most difficult challenges and triumph occurs in Booker T. Washington's account of his emotions and thoughts when he received a letter from Harvard. The letter informed him of their desire to award him an honorary Master of Arts degree.

This was a recognition that had never in the slightest manner entered into my mind, and it was hard for me to realize that I was to be honored by a degree from the oldest and most renowned university in America. As I sat upon my veranda, with this letter in my hand, tears came to my eyes. My whole former life—my life as a slave on the plantation, my work in the coal-mine, the times when I was without food and clothing, when I made my bed under a sidewalk, my struggles for an education, the trying days I had had at Tuskegee, days when I did not know where to turn for a dollar to continue the work there, the ostracism and sometimes oppression of my race,—all this passed before me and nearly overcame me.[1]

This identity had been formed and purified in the crucible and "school" of slavery and racism.[2] This identity had the liberating and healing force of God. It was indomitable: neither the terror of lynching nor the sting of a whip could take it away. Not even hunger and cold could break it. It was uplifting. It made people rise.

This identity was something so noble that it made American civilization a more noble society. It had the force of justice and truth, and the force to empower progress. It is an identity that black Americans need to reclaim.

MISEDUCATION AND EDUTAINMENT

Another problem is that young black Americans do not always make the connection between their conservative insights into life (the things their parents and grandparents taught them) and the Republican philosophy. I see two reasons for this: (1) lack of an effective Republican outreach and (2) the misunderstood character of the Democratic and Republican parties. But this situation is changing.

Peer pressure is the greatest challenge; it is intimidating. The fear of being alienated by peers keeps many black college students from joining the ranks of the Republican party. In fact, my personal experiences in being both black and Republican could make for a volume of anecdotes. I have faced angry students who were angry not about my ideas but because I called myself a Republican. I think it takes courage and self-honesty. Without these virtues, wrong choices are made in the face of difficult choices.

"Edutainment" and "gangsta" rap has not helped young men and women make good choices either. In fact, "gangsta" rap and the conspiracy theories that pass as rap confuse important distinctions. Suspicion is presented as knowledge. Booker T. Washington didn't feel that way when he accepted his honorary degree from Harvard in 1896. Of course, Harvard was a decent school in those days.

In fact, Washington's impression of the people in attendance at the ceremony and what was happening there would be shocking to the purveyors of "edutainment" such as Ice Cube who always has something bad to say about the "System." Washington's pride in being part of the ceremony shines through his description. "To see over a thousand strong men, representing all that is best in State, Church, business, and education, with the glow of college loyalty and college pride,—which has, I think, a peculiar Harvard flavor,—is a sight that does not easily fade from memory."[3]

LOOKING FOR SIGNS OF FRIENDSHIP

Not all black students are deceived—only some. In my experience, no matter what university I am visiting, I always find several students who are also black and Republican. Of course, most students do not make public confessions of these private sentiments. They fear the backlash of misguided activists who believe that liberal groupthink provides identity and the means to empowerment. Often, their fear is substantiated. The threats against the life of black conservative collegian Mark Hardie and his family in California are testament of the trial that young, black Republicans must undergo if they vocalize their position.

Although the need for outreach is not the greatest problem, the courage to be oneself without fear and embarrassment can be nourished by friendship. I do believe that if the GOP were to make a more concentrated effort to listen to the concerns of blacks, black Americans would respond. If Republican outreach to the black community were to become an important issue for the party, and if Republican officials would spend far more time listening to black constituents, I predict that popular black opinion would make a permanent shift away from the Democratic party.

The misunderstanding is slowly clearing up through the efforts of African-American groups like Minority Mainstream, the New Coalition for Economic and Social Change, and Project 21. These organizations are challenging the half-truths spun by the press and the old guard of the civil rights establishment. Republican party outreach to the African-American community is improving slowly, particularly through the work of groups like College Republican National Committee (CRNC) and Empower America.

When I first met the chairman of the CRNC, Bill Spadea, he expressed a concern for the problem that conservative ideas were not getting out to African Americans. More importantly, he believed that black Americans in the Republican party should be seen not as black Republicans but as individuals. Where is the logic in defining individuals by their ethnicity?

DON'T MISS THE BUS

Building confidence between Republicans and black Americans must be attempted at many levels. Without such warm communication, the Republican party cannot successfully represent the American people—all the American people. But the need for outreach is not the greatest challenge that black Americans face when deciding on their political identity. Sometimes, black conservatives have to be patient.

The signs of friendship can sometimes seem too few and too little. Jack Kemp was right about the Republican party missing the bus during the civil rights movement. It also seems to me that Republicans missed the bus in the best years: the Reagan years. But the bus keeps coming back. One of these days, we are going to get the Republican party on that bus.

We have seen excellent examples of such a shift in the elections of Republicans Bret Schundler, mayor of Jersey City, Christine Whitman, governor of New Jersey, and Richard Riordan, mayor of Los Angeles. We have already seen turnarounds in the 1994 November elections. The turnaround happened in part because black Americans are interested in overcoming the same challenges that all Americans face in pursuing the American dream.

Black Americans have begun to recognize there is a realism and scope of multidimensional insight to conservative thinking. They are rethinking ideas in a realistic manner. It is a realism that is lacking in the tired, liberal platitudes advocated by the civil rights establishment. Indeed, conservative thought has enabled me to envision a new destiny for black Americans.

NOTES

1. Booker T. Washington, *Up from Slavery* (New York: Oxford University Press, 1995), 174.

2. Ibid., 9. Washington writes: "We must acknowledge that, not-withstanding the cruelty and moral wrong of slavery, the ten million Negroes inhabiting this country, who themselves or whose ancestors went through the school of slavery, are in a stronger and more hopeful condition, materially, intellectually, morally, and religiously, than is true of an equal number of black people in any other portion of the globe." It also seems obvious that the school of slavery made black Americans who were more moral, more religious, and more wise than their masters.

3. Ibid., 175.

5

WHAT "BLACK CONSERVATIVE" MEANS TO ME

Lee Walker

There is [a] class of [black] people who make a business of keeping the troubles, the wrongs, the hardships of the Negro race before the public. Having learned that they are able to make a living out of their troubles, they have grown into the settled habit of advertising their wrongs—partly because they want sympathy, and partly because it pays.

Booker T. Washington

What does it mean if you are an American black and are described as a "conservative"? Unfortunately, the word "conservative" almost uniformly calls up negative stereotypes in the black community. But to my mind, the word is best used as an adjective, not a noun, for it seems to me that conservatism is best understood as a state of mind and type of character, a way of looking at the social order.

BOOKER T. WASHINGTON

My thinking on black conservatism begins primarily with the writings of Booker T. Washington. He saw the solution to the problem of black progress clearer than any of his critics. He argued that economic progress held the key to advancement in every area of life, and so he heroically struggled to improve himself, to be qualified to excel.

But after Washington's death in 1915, his image among black Americans was seriously diminished. This was not justified, and as Thomas Sowell wrote in the December 1994 issue of *Forbes* magazine, the Booker-bashing was one of the most unfair hands dealt to any black leader in the history of this country. How ironic that Booker T. Washington, a man of such great intellect and accomplishment, a giant of his time, would be so villainized, and largely by other blacks. Have they forgotten that this self-made man was the first black American on a U.S. coin; on a postage stamp; to be invited to dinner by a U.S. president; to have tea with the queen of England; to have a battleship as well as schools across the country named after him? Furthermore, Washington graduated with honors from Hampton University, taught there, was a married man who raised a family, delivered a commencement speech at Harvard and was awarded an honorary M.A. degree from that school, as well as an honorary doctorate from Dartmouth.

The next time you are in New York City, visit the great Riverside Church in upper Manhattan. To the right side of Christ hanging high over the altar are three statues. They are General Samuel Armstrong, founder of Hampton University, Abraham Lincoln, and Booker T. Washington. For those today who wonder about what conservative blacks want to conserve, they will find the answer in the fierce determination of Booker T.'s stare: diligence, character, integrity, faith in this country. As with Frederick Douglass before him and Lincoln after him, Washington had the ideas, strategy, and skill to influence the behavior of black and white Americans. Washington was a political realist, and he worked to improve society, including race relations, to the degree he could. His wisdom is patent still today, and all Americans would do well to consult him and so further his legacy.

CHARACTER

One of the lessons Washington—and black conservatives generally—would bring us today is the centrality of character. Despite all our rhetoric, we have forgotten this. But black conservatives are working to remind our country of this critical point. That is perhaps their great contribution to our civic life.

In retrospect, for much of my life I had never considered myself a conservative. I, like the rest of my friends, had a strong interest in equal opportunity and was involved in civil rights work during the mid-1950s through the 1960s. My first experience as a community activist began during the period of the Montgomery bus boycott. Moving to New York City during the early 1960s, I witnessed the New York City riots. I was vice president of the Brooklyn, New York, chapter of the NAACP. But in 1980, thanks to the growing prominence of the work of people like Thomas Sowell, I at last had a chance to break a self-imposed censorship on controversial topics and remarks, and to talk openly with others about the centrality of character and values, and the disappointment so many black Americans feel with their de facto "leaders."

It was a liberating experience, one I hope others will come to share as we move into the twenty-first century. This, in my view, is the promise and significance of contemporary black conservatism.

II

PERSPECTIVES ON POLITICS

Throughout this decade, the political critique of black conservatives has been gaining strength and attention. In place of the conventional and now anachronistic, race-conscious, government-based "program" approach to black empowerment, the black conservative would substitute an emphasis on individualist, entrepreneurial self-reliance and personal diligence.

Part II presents a sampling of this critique that has so altered the dynamics of recent political and racial discourse. In Chapter 6 Brian W. Jones conducts an analysis of these two styles of black leadership, contrasting the civil rights paradigm—derived from the legacy of W.E.B. Du Bois—with an approach representative of black conservatism that can be traced to the thought of Booker T. Washington. In Chapter 7 Willie and Gwen Richardson examine the puzzling persistence of the American media culture's continuing underrecognition of the force and prevalence of black conservatism. While progress in this area has been made, equal time is still not a reality. Chapter 8 presents Telly Lovelace's observations on the powerful work ethic and tradition of self-sufficiency that has infused black history. Chapter 9 gives voice to Mazhar Ali Awan's vigorous call for educational achievement in urban black communities, and Chapter 10 offers former Congressman Gary Franks's agenda for black conservative advocacy.

These essays demonstrate why the political voice of black conservatives is on an upward trajectory, and why, as the politics of the new millennium takes shape, it is certain to be a formative influence.

6

TWO VISIONS OF BLACK LEADERSHIP

Brian W. Jones

Visions set the agenda for both thought and action.
                                        Thomas Sowell, economist

The year 1991 was a watershed in the competition for the public leadership of African-American communities. In the summer of that year, President George Bush nominated Circuit Court Judge Clarence Thomas as his choice to succeed the legendary Thurgood Marshall on the United States Supreme Court. Whatever the president's intentions in selecting Judge Thomas, his nomination underscored in stark relief the competing visions of leadership which today confront black Americans.

MARSHALL AND THOMAS

Thurgood Marshall, a scion of the early legacy of W.E.B. Du Bois, represented the civil rights era paradigm that identified institutionalized white racism as the foremost obstacle to black social progress. Accordingly, improvement of conditions for blacks necessitates an emphasis on political rights, bureaucratic paternalism, and the intellectual development of the black elite, or in Du Bois's phrase, "the talented tenth." It is a philosophy that speaks less to the need for individual and community empowerment than for legal efforts and centralized, governmental action.

Clarence Thomas, on the other hand, a man of Horatio Alger-like ascendancy, has chosen to grace the walls of his chambers with portraits of Booker T. Washington. And for good reason. Washington, a contemporary and rival of Du Bois, believed that economic empowerment and self-reliance were the *sine qua non* of civic progress. As a corollary to that proposition, Washington agreed that blacks must cultivate the personal and civic virtues that make economic success possible. For example, the National Negro Business League, which Washington helped found in 1900, adopted as its principal objectives (1) the development of "high character"; (2) the development of "racial respect"; (3) the development of "economic stability" (viz., personal industry); and (4) the laying of an "economic groundwork for future generations" (viz., thrift and investment).[1] Without such virtues, Washington argued, the DuBoisian emphasis on political progress would ultimately prove illusory for the less talented nine-tenths.

These two competing—albeit, at times complementary—leadership paradigms are at the very core of the political struggle in the black community today. The prevailing African-American leadership inherits from the civil rights generation a profound belief in the pervasiveness and "institutionalization" of white racism in America. Accordingly, its lodestar is a paternalistic statism that serves ostensibly to "protect" its clients from unfair treatment.

The insurgent neo-Washingtonian model of leadership, on the other hand, responds not to the perceived limitations of the American system, but rather to the real opportunities extant within it—opportunities that in substantial part owe their existence to the victories of the civil rights movement. Thus, it may be said that while the civil rights movement opened the door of progress to African Americans, the question remains whether black leadership in the 1990s struggles simply to open the door even wider or whether it prepares all African Americans to take a step across the threshold.

That the competition of visions is approaching the vibrancy it enjoyed at the turn of the century, however, dates roughly to the moment of Clarence Thomas's Supreme Court nomination. That event not only brought to public light the existence of considerable black dissent from the statist status quo, but it also made plain that the self-reliance strategies and community empowerment efforts of black conservatives resonated to the grassroots black community.

The genesis of these yearnings cannot, of course, be attributed solely to the Thomas nomination. Rather, the nomination coincided with the rejection of political leftism throughout the world and in the larger American society in particular. This rejection was precipitated by the perceived deterioration of America's moral values, personal safety, and economic prospects, as well as bureaucratic liberalism's failure to effectively confront that deterioration.

NEW CONCERNS

What the atmosphere surrounding the Thomas nomination unsheathed in particular, however, was that the black community, while perhaps not prepared to embrace Republicanism or the white conservatives who carry its banner, was searching for a leadership paradigm distinct from the conventional civil rights-era model. Black Americans, like other Americans, sense the distinctly moral dimension of the problems confronting them and increasingly yearn for a leadership model that speaks to that dimension. The question for conservatives, then, is whether blacks can interpret mainstream conservative principles as responding to that yearning. Recent events suggest that the opportunity is lurking.

On October 16, 1995, several hundred thousand black American men gathered in the shadow of the U.S. Capitol building ostensibly to atone for past sins and to take responsibility for their own lives, their families, and their communities. That so-called Million Man March underscored the paradigm shift that was underway among African Americans. Many of the black men who massed outside the Capitol on that day hungered for what a majority of voters demanded from those inside the Capitol in the historic elections of November 1994: individual and community empowerment.

Polls show that a growing proportion of blacks reject the notion that white racism represents the largest obstacle to black civic progress. Rather, they define their communities' problems in economic and spiritual terms. In short, rank-and-file African Americans seem impatient to step through the door of opportunity opened by an earlier generation. That partly explains the attraction of hundreds of thousands of black men to the Million Man March's advertised call to individual responsibility and empowerment. That shift, however, also suggests a more fundamental rejection of conventional civil rights era politics.

The civil rights movement of the 1950s and 1960s was unquestionably an essential phase of the African-American struggle for civic equality. Without equality under law, moral and civic equality are unattainable. Indeed, the political determination to rid us of state-sanctioned discrimination appreciably improved the racial attitudes of individual Americans. That said, it is also true that government cannot make us equal; it can only make us equal before the law. The Du Bois paradigm of leadership, however, rejects that notion; the neo-Washingtonian paradigm, or modern black conservatism, embraces it.

But if government cannot make us equal, what will? The evidence shows that Washington was correct in his belief that economic development—or more importantly, the cultural values that undergird it—is the surer path to moral and civic progress.

The pronouncements of *Brown v. Board of Education* and the passage of the Civil Rights Act of 1964 and the Voting Rights Act of 1965 (the most palpable legacies of the civil rights movement) did improve racial attitudes among white Americans, but much remains to be done. For example, one-third of black children continue to live in poverty, and the overall poverty rate among blacks remains around 31 percent.[2] These figures are not very different from those in 1965. The problems of drug use, crime, and family dissolution have also worsened since the 1960s in the black community, just as they have in the white community.

The leading economic and cultural indicators in the black community worry African Americans today, and there is a growing apprehension that the black community is not in control of its economic destiny. That is, many African Americans believe that as a result of the political and judicial efforts waged by leaders of the civil rights paradigm, so-called black institutions have suffered some erosion.

For example, blacks own fewer banks today than they did during the period 1888–1934.[3] Similarly, fewer blacks are employed by black-owned insurance companies today than were in 1937.[4] Moreover, African Americans who live in blighted urban neighborhoods often find members of other ethnic groups establishing profitable businesses in those neighborhoods, seemingly to the exclusion of black-owned establishments. Each of these facts contributes to the widely held belief that African Americans have lost control of their economic destiny. But because the prevailing leadership of the black community remains obsessed with the blight of racism, it is ill-suited to address the contemporary hopes and fears of the rank and file. By its persistent, almost pathological, exaltation of racism as the fundamental impediment of black progress, the leadership shifts to outside forces the responsibility for problems confronting blacks. Thus, without a sense of personal responsibility for one's own destiny, there is no incentive for individual initiative. Ultimately, then, the black youth asked, Why make the sacrifice to improve my own life if someone else's actions will ultimately determine my fate? That is the question the civil rights era leadership cannot answer.

CONSERVATIVE ACTIVISM

The neo-Washingtonians and many of their conservative allies, however, are poised to speak to the African American's yearning for empowerment. In particular, three spheres of conservative activism appeal quite constructively to that impulse: market-oriented reform of public education; effective crime control; and welfare reform and family restoration strategies.

Education

Educational achievement is an essential component of upward mobility in America. The statistics are telling: while in the aggregate blacks tend to earn less than whites, controlling for educational achievement reveals that the disparity is closing rapidly, and that indeed, in some cases it has closed together. For example, the Census Bureau reports that in 1993, black men with college degrees working in managerial jobs earned 86 percent of what similarly situated white men earned.[5] Black women with college degrees in managerial jobs actually earned on average 10 percent more than their white counterparts.[6]

The centrality of education to socioeconomic progress in the United States underscores the tragedy of our primary and secondary public education system, particularly our urban public school systems. In California, only 5 percent of black public high school graduates and 4 percent of Hispanic public high school graduates meet the minimum course and grade requirements for admission to the University of California.[7] In inner-city Milwaukee, Wisconsin, the public school system has a graduation rate of only 48 percent; the dropout rate in that system is seven times the statewide average; and 79 percent of entering seniors in Milwaukee public schools failed a math proficiency exam required for graduation. By contrast, the nine private high schools in inner-city Milwaukee boast a 96 percent attendance rate and an 88 percent graduation rate.[8]

Moreover, despite the battle cry of the education establishment—and its supporters among the civil rights era black leadership—lack of resources is rarely at fault. Parochial schools in cities around the nation generally do a better job of educating students, at lower cost, than large, urban public school districts. In short, our public school systems are failing those who are most vulnerable in our society, those without options. The conventional black leadership, however, is reluctant to provide those options. It remains ever statist in its approach, arguing yet again for greater "resources" to be paid to state education bureaucrats.

Neo-Washingtonians then have an opportunity to speak to the yearnings of average black citizens for individual control over the education of their children. Indeed, the school choice initiatives now underway in cities like Milwaukee and those soon to be launched in Cleveland, Ohio, and Washington, D.C., are truly efforts at individual and community empowerment. They seek to give parents and families the opportunity to control their own destinies. The ultimate evidence of the desire for control is the fact that 88 percent of African Americans who are aware of school choice initiatives approve of them.[9]

Crime

Crime is impeding the upward mobility of a great many African Americans. In 1995, according to the Federal Bureau of Investigation, fourteen million "major crimes" were committed in the United States (566 crimes per 10,000 citizens). Moreover, crime victimization rates in the United States are inversely related to the income level of victims. That is to say, the poorer one is, the more likely he or she is to be a victim of crime.[10] Law-abiding citizens living in economically distressed, predominantly black, urban areas have been particularly hard hit by the pathologies of crime and drugs—so much so that many of them are prepared to sacrifice precious liberties to live in some modicum of peace. For example, witness the recent efforts of poor inner-city residents to reclaim their public housing complexes from drug peddlers and violent thugs. The housing authorities in several of America's largest cities have proposed broad, warrantless sweeps of public housing projects in an effort to rid those communities of the drugs and guns that ravage the lives of the law-abiding. In San Francisco, a private security firm was hired to carry out such measures at the Geneva Gardens housing project. While once reputed as San Francisco's most dangerous housing project, reports of crime fell by 45 percent during the first year of the security detail, and in 1994, not one "major crime" report was filed from the project.

That conscientious citizens should feel compelled to sacrifice some of their liberty to live in peace is a tragedy of leadership. This is particularly so given the conventional black leadership's statist obsession with procedural protections for accused victimizers and its incessant efforts to rationalize the victimizer's behavior with arguments about racism and economic determinism. Of course, all of that talk is of little importance to the child who is unable to play outside with his friends, or the grandmother who cowers behind bolted doors and windows for fear of the dangers ever present in the public square.

Thus again, the neo-Washingtonians and their conservative allies have an opportunity to empower individuals and communities by allowing them to reassert authority over their neighborhoods and their streets. By dealing forthrightly with crime by emphasizing the incapacitation (viz., incarceration) of victimizers, and by exhibiting a determination to confront family dissolution (which is the truest "root cause" of crime), communities can be free to exercise the self-determination that is at the root of the American dream.

Welfare Reform and Family Restoration

If educational failure and crime are two fundamental obstacles to civic progress, the problem of family dissolution is the foundation on which each of them stands. And the welfare system serves to exacerbate the rate of that dissolution.

Like educational achievement, family status is a substantial determinant of one's socioeconomic status. Recent studies have shown that black families headed by two married parents earn a median income that is only 1 percent below the average income for all families and 88 percent that of comparable white families.[11] Strong families—which are less a function of bureaucratic government than of individual effort and community reinforcement—are apparently the cornerstone of civic equality.

To the extent that the incentives of the welfare system marginalize or even obviate the role of men as breadwinners and essential components of viable family units, it must be substantially reformed. As long as public policy undermines the economic rationale for marriage, communities will be powerless to confront very real impediments to socioeconomic mobility.

A CROSSROADS

What all this suggests is that African Americans have reached an important crossroads of public leadership. Although many blacks have begun to question the efficacy of a statist leadership that appears unable to forge a new strategy to recover the moral and economic legacy of our history in America, they have yet to embrace conservatism as an alternative. The neo-Washingtonians, however, have yet to forcefully make their case. While the Thomas nomination underscored the contrasting visions of leadership and energized a younger generation of neo-Washingtonians, much remains to be said about the nexus between self-reliance as an ideology and the black community's yearning for self-determination. By emphasizing—via the advocacy of school choice, criminal incapacitations, and family restoration strategies—individual and community ability to improve their status without bureaucratic intervention, neo-Washingtonians may seize a brief moment of opportunity and win the loyalty of average blacks. In so doing, they will have rejected the notion, embraced by the tired civil rights paradigm of leadership, that institutionalized inequalities pervade the American system and thus preclude blacks from enjoying real opportunities for upward mobility. The result of that rejection will be a reaffirmation of the promise of America, which in turn will ultimately be to the socioeconomic benefit of African Americans, as well as to the moral and civic benefit of all Americans.

NOTES

1. John Sibley Butler, *Entrepreneurship and Self-Help among Black Americans: A Reconsideration of Race and Economics* (Albany, N.Y.: State University of New York Press, 1991), 67.

2. Glenn C. Loury, "Not-so Black and White: The Two Americas Are Actually Converging," *Washington Post*, 15 October 1995, C3.

3. Butler, *Entrepreneurship and Self-Help among Black Americans*, 303.

4. Ibid., 309.

5. Loury, "Not-so Black and White: The Two Americas Are Actually Converging," C3.

6. Ibid.

7. Remarks of Jack Peltason, president of the University of California, to the Board of Regents, July 20, 1995.

8. "Memorandum of Interenors/Defendants, Parents for School Choice et al., In Opposition to Motions for Temporary Injunction, State ex rel. *Tommy G. Thompson v. Jackson*, Supreme Court of Wisconsin," Case no. 95–215–OA.

9. Tamar Jacoby, "A Whole Different Crop of Black Leaders," *City Journal* (summer 1995): 26.

10. William J. Bennett, *The Index of Leading Cultural Indicators: Facts and Figures on the State of American Society* (New York: Simon and Schuster, 1994), 19–20.

11. Abigail Thernstrom and Stephan Thernstrom, "The Promise of Racial Equality," in *The New Promise of American Life*, Lamar Alexander and Chester E. Finn, Jr., eds. (Indianapolis, Ind.: The Hudson Institute, 1995), 91.

7

BLACK CONSERVATIVES: THE UNDERCOUNTED

Willie and Gwen Richardson

National media tend to downplay or even ignore the gathering momentum that [black conservatives] are enjoying. This view stems from [the fact] they are ideologically disinclined to recognize the potential self-sufficiency of the poor.
Robert L. Woodson

Contrary to popular belief, conservative values are not anathema to a large number of black Americans. In fact, blacks who identify themselves as conservative have been a substantial force since at least the early 1990s, according to four separate national opinion surveys.

A series of *Washington Post* polls conducted in 1991 found that among 455 blacks surveyed, 35 percent identified themselves as "conservative" or "very conservative." The next year, in 1992, the Washington D.C.-based Joint Center for Political and Economic Studies conducted a poll in which 33 percent of blacks surveyed said they were conservative.

This rightward trend may be even more pronounced in the South. A 1994 Rice University survey of black Houstonians revealed that 38 percent admitted they were conservative. And in 1995 the Texas office of the National Association for the Advancement of Colored People polled black Texans and found that 40 percent considered themselves conservative, reinforcing the findings of the three other polls.

If so many blacks say they are conservative, then where are they? Why don't we hear more from them in the media?

REASONS FOR OBSCURITY

There are several reasons why they are hidden. One is that blacks may be more willing to admit they are conservative in the privacy of their own homes, under the cover of anonymity provided by the opinion poll. But the most compelling reason is that black conservatives may be the only blacks in the United States who are not protected by the rules of due process or even basic civility. Apparently, *ad hominem* attacks on the personal character of blacks who dare announce their conservatism are not only tolerated, but are also expected and enthusiastically issued. Since no one wants to be subjected to the vicious name-calling and reckless falsehoods that black conservatives encounter on a regular basis, many blacks with these dissident rightward views would rather stay in the closet with their opinions—even though these opinions are traditional in nature—than endure the epithets.

For example, the June 26, 1995, edition of *Time* magazine included an article on Supreme Court Justice Clarence Thomas entitled "Uncle Tom Justice." The writer of this article, Jack E. White, described Thomas as "the scariest of all the [Washington, D.C.] hobgoblins." White, like many reporters writing about black conservatives, freely performed some makeshift psychoanalysis on the associate justice, saying "The most disturbing thing about Thomas is not his conclusions, but his twisted reasoning and bilious rage."

Can you imagine the outcry if Jesse Jackson or a Democratic member of the Congressional Black Caucus had been similarly vilified in the press? The media obviously believe their unrestrained attacks on black conservatives will go unanswered, and in the main they do go unanswered.

But bomb throwers won't be able to continue for long. There is a burgeoning movement of young black conservatives who are aggressively organizing at the grassroots level, and their impact will surely be felt. While their influence is mounting, many of them have held conservative views all their lives. But many seem to have had some sort of defining experience that led them in that direction.

For some, the issue of abortion was the catalyst. As pro-life Christians, they cannot countenance the liberal politics that degrades unborn human life and views it as expendable. For others, the Clarence Thomas confirmation hearings were an eye-opener, as they saw conservatives go all-out for their nominee, something rarely done by liberals, who tend to dump their black political appointees as soon as the going gets tough—remember Lani Guinier and Dr. Henry Foster? For still others, the liberals' paternalistic attitude toward black Americans as a whole—viewing them only as victims and not as independent persons who can chart their own course—was the final straw.

Whatever the motivation, a sizable proportion of black Americans no longer want to align themselves with liberal politicians and policies. Many observers misinterpret this phenomenon. It does not necessarily mean that large numbers of blacks will declare themselves to be Republican. The terms *conservative* and *Republican* are not always interchangeable. But there is a significant shift toward independent voting among black Americans.

The Harris organization polled black voters in April 1995 and found that 31 percent said they were independent, while only 61 percent said they were solid Democrats. Three years earlier, a Joint Center survey had found that only 23 percent of blacks called themselves independent. An increase in independent voting is usually a sign of either an impending switch in political party affiliation or a willingness to vote for candidates based on the issues rather than purely party considerations.

ROADBLOCKS

Still, certain obstacles may thwart this general conservative trend. First, the actions that some conservatives take in determining public policy, especially concerning issues that directly affect black citizens, often send a signal that some motives are tinged with racism. Recent Supreme Court decisions on affirmative action and majority-black districts add to the sense that some want to turn back the clock on civil rights gains.

Second, the liberal media are actively engaged in efforts to discredit black conservatives, whenever practical, by portraying them as pawns of the Republican party. Third, liberal black leaders see the advent of conservative views as a threat to their decades-old stronghold on the black vote and are set to wage a determined fight to maintain that control. Finally, some black conservatives, though well-intentioned, could do a better job of presenting their views. Their strident stances often make them appear insensitive.

Even with these obstacles, in the future, more and more black Americans will adopt myriad conservative approaches to problem solving. This social phenomenon will occur out of political necessity. Old liberal solutions—which are increasingly becoming anachronistic and ineffectual—simply have not worked.

8

NO NEED FOR A GOVERNMENT HANDOUT

Telly Lovelace

If we had to name the one institution that has been the enemy of humankind, it would be governments around the world, including our own. . . . A certain amount of [government] is necessary . . . [but] [o]ur federal government is increasingly becoming destructive of the ends it was created to serve.

Walter E. Williams, economist

Government control has diverted the black American community from the road of prosperity and good fortune to the road of government dependency. However, this has not always been the case. Free markets and entrepreneurship have historically offered black Americans a solution to the catastrophe created by government intervention—whether motivated by racism or by a desire to help.

FREE MARKETS AND ENTREPRENEURSHIP

Historically, the black community has prospered most when it has embraced free markets and entrepreneurship. Black Americans have advanced by embracing these institutions despite slavery, segregation, Jim Crow laws, and various forms of well-meaning but addled government assistance.

Today, it seems that government control has intruded into virtually all elements of the everyday lives of black Americans. These regulations and controls affect their lives economically, socially, politically, and psychologically. For example, the current welfare state has helped destroy many black families by taking wage-earning fathers out of homes and replacing them with a monthly government check. Black Americans, though just 12 percent of the population, currently make up more than one-third of the entire welfare system in the United States.

Even so, black Americans have historically risen above the collective handouts of the government and into a state of personal responsibility by actively participating in a free market system that promotes the spirit of self-help. This habit of black entrepreneurship can be traced back to the pre-Civil War period. Black-owned businesses during this period were divided into two categories: those comprised of freed blacks and those made up of slaves who participated in business enterprises.

EXAMPLES

This state of personal responsibility among black Americans was evident during the pre-Civil War period. During the 1820s and 1830s, black Americans were successful in businesses such as sail making, blacksmithing, carpentry, and cabinet making.[1] Blacks also owned businesses in various fields, including real estate, construction, trade, manufacturing, transportation, and merchandising (these businesses were particularly profitable for free black Americans during the pre-Civil War period). Blacks' dominant roles in these businesses are best exemplified by the fact that they employed many white Americans. For example, James Forten ran an influential sail manufacturing company and in 1821, employed more than forty blacks and whites. Stephen Smith matched Forten's entrepreneurial spirit: Smith was a lumber merchant whose annual sales grossed over $100,000 by the mid-nineteenth century. By 1864, Smith's net earnings were placed at $500,000. Both Smith and Forten are good examples of businesses that were lucrative for free black Americans in northern cities.[2]

In addition to northern blacks, enslaved southern blacks took advantage of free enterprise. In 1812, the enslaved man Free Flank hired other slaves from his master and developed a saltpeter (the primary ingredient in gunpowder) factory in Kentucky. As a result of his endeavor, he was able to purchase his wife's freedom in 1817 and his own in 1819, at the cost of $1,600.[3] Many slaves during this same period purchased their freedom. In Ohio, more than one-third of the black slaves purchased their freedom by

1839, at a total cost of $215,000. In 1847, 275 of the 1,077 black slaves in Philadelphia had purchased their freedom for a total cost of $60,000.[4]

At the turn of the century, Jim Crow laws imposed a state of universal segregation throughout the South. This segregation became formalized by the 1896 Supreme Court decision *Plessy v. Ferguson*, which upheld the doctrine of "separate but equal." From this doctrine various Jim Crow laws emerged. These were designed to segregate blacks by economic isolation (an economic "detour" that makes the black experience in America unique).[5]

Jim Crow laws forced businesses in the black community to concentrate into race-exclusive districts. Although blacks resisted the relocation of their businesses to the downtown areas and poorer neighborhoods, they were unsuccessful. Indeed, these laws held them back. In the South, however, the black middle class grew with the availability of land.

Even though black Americans have historically suffered numerous setbacks, their overall economic situation has been one of increasing prosperity over time. Indeed, between 1867 and 1917, the number of black enterprises increased from four thousand to fifty thousand.[6]

Black Americans have historically taken advantage of free markets and have been successful. A perfect example is their free market success in the banking arena of black communities during the Great Depression. Banks in the black community triumphed and overcame the nation's general financial collapse. (This is in contrast to many other banks that failed, and most of these were located in the white community.)

Following the Great Depression, in 1938 black retail merchants annually grossed more than $101 million and employed more than 28,000 proprietors and firm members, as well as 12,561 full-time employees. The total payroll for these retail merchants was more than 8.5 million.[7]

GOVERNMENT HARMS

In 1931, Representative Robert Bacon, a Republican from New York well known for his racist views, and Senator James Davis, a Republican from Pennsylvania, introduced legislation preventing migrant black workers from competing with whites during the Great Depression. The so-called Davis-Bacon Act was racist in its intentions. Representative Bacon drafted this legislation after an Alabama contractor, who employed only black laborers, won a contract for a federal building in Bacon's Long Island district. The act was supported by many white union workers, whose jobs were threatened by skilled, nonunion black workers. This government regulation prevented black-owned construction firms from competing with white firms.[8]

In contrast to the laws designed to detour blacks from prosperity and independence (such as the Jim Crow laws), the well-intentioned federal programs of the New Deal took black Americans into a life of government dependency. It was the first step in the creation of government programs that helped destroy two institutions responsible for black success: work and marriage. The rate of deterioration increased with the introduction of the Great Society by Lyndon Johnson in the mid-1960s.

Johnson's Great Society created still more government programs whose intentions were good but have unfortunately helped destroy the black community. The objective of the Great Society was to end poverty in America. To accomplish this goal, government programs were necessary to assist people to get out of poverty by helping them receive additional funds. But thirty years after the implementation of the Great Society, the black community has both witnessed and suffered the failed "War on Poverty." Today, more than one-third of black Americans make up the welfare state, illegitimacy has skyrocketed among black Americans (as well as whites), and the crime rate is on the rise (especially in the inner cities, which contain the highest concentration of black Americans). For example, in 1965 the illegitimacy rate in the black community stood at 26 percent, but by 1991 had increased to 66.3 percent and it continues rising every year.[9] This has been the result even though the federal government has spent more than $3.5 trillion on the War on Poverty since 1965. In addition, counting state and local spending, $5 trillion have been squandered on the welfare state.[10] Despite increased welfare spending and illegitimacy, the crime rate has more than tripled since 1960.[11] These statistics are particularly ironic considering that many Great Society programs were originally designed to curb the crime rate (especially in inner cities like Washington, D.C.). Yet, the "nation's capital" is one of the least safe cities in the country, and until recently its crime rate continued to rise every year.

The 1980s offered a cure for the virus of government dependency created by politicians over the past thirty years: free enterprise. Rigorous free enterprise has been documented to increase business and employment in the black community. During the 1980s the number of black firms rose 38 percent from 308,000 to 424,000. This was accomplished through self-empowerment instead of government handouts. Most of these successes were wrought through local, community-based programs. In addition, more blacks were hired during the 1980s. Black unemployment dropped from 20.4 percent in December 1982 to 11.4 percent in 1989.[12]

Despite government programs intervening on behalf of (yet ultimately harming) the black community, blacks have always prospered. Furthermore, despite the historical hardships of slavery, the Jim Crow laws, and segregation, black Americans have always been able to succeed through their sense of self-initiative. The formula for black American success with free enterprise is simple: it requires the ingenuity of the human mind, the courage of the human heart, and the creativity of the human spirit. But the government, through its activism, saps these resources, bringing about the unintended consequences of idleness, dependency, and a debilitating mindset of entitlement.

NOTES

1. John Sibley Butler, *Entrepreneurship and Self-Help among Black Americans* (Albany, N.Y.: State University of New York Press, 1991).

2. Ibid.

3. Ibid.

4. Ibid.

5. Ibid.

6. Ibid.

7. Ibid.

8. Horace Cooper and Ronald Nehring, "Government Bureaucracy versus Economic Development," in *Black America 1994: Changing Direction* (Washington, D.C.: National Center for Public Policy Research, 1994).

9. William J. Bennett, *The Index of Leading Cultural Indicators* (New York: Simon and Schuster, 1994).

10. Peter Kirsanow, "Welfare Reform: An Emancipation Proclamation for the Twentieth Century," in *Black America 1995: A New Beginning* (Washington, D.C.: National Center for Public Policy Research, 1995).

11. Scott A. Hodge, *Crime Rates and Welfare Spending* (Washington, D.C.: Heritage Foundation, 1994).

12. Project 21 Data Sheet, "Trickle-Down Economics Worked" (Washington, D.C.: National Center for Public Policy Research, 1994).

9

EDUCATIONAL DEVELOPMENT IN THE BLACK COMMUNITY

Mazhar Ali Awan

*Investment in human potential and in people is far more important than invest-
ment in bricks and mortar. Educating the people must take priority over the
building of dams and factories.*

Moeen A. Qureshi

The development of any race, clan, family, nation, state, town, village, or
ghetto is integrally tied to the level of education its people achieve. As most
economists agree, human resources, not capital or natural resources, ultimately determine the pace of socioeconomic development. The "economic
returns to schooling" are extremely important to both the individual and the
country as a whole.[1] The economic principles are poignant and many statistics prove this point over and over again, but most black Americans, particularly in the inner city, seem to ignore them.

The first step to achieving socioeconomic development is good education.
It is difficult to run a cash register if you do not have a fundamental understanding of arithmetic. It is difficult to stock inventories if you do not know
how to read an order form, and even more so if you cannot write. Fundamental as this sounds, a whole generation of inner-city youth fits this description.

Examining schooling as it affects the supply and demand curves of the labor market, it is obvious that an increase in the demand for more educated workers implies an increase in the compensation for educated workers. Conversely, a decline in demand for less schooled workers implies a decline in the wages of less schooled workers—in the long run. In fact, the U.S. economy has been demanding more and more educated workers in recent years.

The Third World has been particularly receptive to the idea that education is the first step to development. Some Third World countries spend as much as 30 percent of their total recurrent government revenues on education.[2] These countries are paying the high cost of education without complaint because they realize that the lag time for educational development to affect the economy is twenty to twenty-five years.

This lag time in the educational impact on economic improvement is not true, however, for black Americans. Black Americans are not challenged by the absence of broad infrastructures and essential institutions as in most Third World countries. They live in a developed country whose political structure encourages individual prosperity. It seems that those living in the inner city too often cry wolf when they criticize their educational resources. Whether they are correct will have to be flushed out in the "issues" that define the obstacles said to exist.

UNSAFE SCHOOLS, UNEQUAL STANDARDS

The students are not safe in many inner-city schools. The solution to this problem includes students and parents, not simply throwing more money at the problem. For example, students must band together and help the administration identify troublemakers. Parents also have to take responsibility for their children. If a child is bringing a gun to school, both the student and parents should be penalized. Every parent understands that inherent responsibilities come with raising a child; there can be no excuses to the contrary. Just because both parents work to make ends meet, that does not absolve them of their responsibility for their children and the safety of other children. When the people finally take ownership of their schools, an environment suitable to learning will be established, and no amount of funding can by itself remedy the problem.

Beyond the essentiality for parental involvement and accountability, professional "educrats" in the black community frequently argue that the quality of inner-city education is not equal to the suburban school setting, and therefore black students simply cannot succeed. But this point is unsubstantiated. The minimum qualifications for teachers are the same throughout the country. Still, if a city so desires, it always has the option to raise standards for its system. Parents and students alike can urge their school system to do the same; there is nothing stopping them from doing this. At any rate, nearly all higher educational institutions have special allowances for graduates of inner-city schools, and a diligent student can take advantage of these programs. In addition, all colleges and universities are legally bound to provide for equal opportunity. Most colleges and universities only require a Scholastic Aptitude Test score and proof of good performance in high school. These are simple requirements that any serious-minded student can achieve, even if faced with adverse circumstances.

ACHIEVEMENT

Obviously, these so-called issues are just excuses. Many social scientists point to other minorities who have come to America and flourished. For example, consider the following comparisons of educational achievement by race and sex for 1990 and 1991 (complete data are available only for these years).[3]

PERCENTAGE COMPLETED HIGH SCHOOL

	White		Black		Asian	
	M	F	M	F	M	F
1990	79.1	79.0	65.8	66.5	84.0	77.2
1991	79.8	79.9	66.7	66.7	83.8	80.0

PERCENTAGE COMPLETED COLLEGE

	White		Black		Asian	
	M	F	M	F	M	F
1990	25.3	19.0	11.9	10.8	44.9	35.4
1991	25.4	19.3	11.4	11.6	43.2	35.5

As the table shows, the high school completion rate is significantly lower for black students. The most startling statistics are in the second half of the table: 44.9 percent of Asian males completed four years of college in 1990. These students are well ahead of even white students at 25.3 percent, even though they may face greater obstacles to education in terms of language. These statistics relate to how well each of these groups is being compensated in the real business world. The median income in current dollars for white, black, and Asian households in 1993 was $32,960, $19,533, and $38,347, respectively.[4] These figures show a dramatic disparity. But the disparity is the result not of racism, as is usually claimed, but of differences in levels of education. Again, the reality is that true hard work cannot be thwarted.

The concept of opportunity costs needs to be emphasized in the inner city. The long-term investment required has been forgotten for the short-term fix or the easy road—often a road that leads straight to jail. For example, a high school dropout working at McDonald's makes $4.25 per hour for an eight-hour day equaling $34.00 in total pay. When the same McDonald's employee sees other dropouts making $5,000 a day selling drugs and not even breaking a sweat, the belief that hard work pays off loses its efficacy. The failure to realize the long- and short-term cost of selling drugs and pursuing other criminal ventures is the problem for most people going in and out of the penal system. Costs such as shorter lifespan, constant danger, threat of gang wars, arrest by police, jailing, and the dissolution of family do not seem to be counted. But ultimately, the choice is simple: if you choose to drop out of school, then you have to learn to live within your means and morally deal with the consequences.

What more proof does a young child need of the benefits of staying in school than to see a friend or classmate die at so young an age? Perhaps the real problem is not "society," but the human capital problem of the lack of goals or ability to morally negotiate goals. Most children do have an idea of what they want to be when they grow up, or, at least, what they would like to get out of life. This is a beginning to work with, though as is often the case those aspirations will undergo many transformations over the years. With help from the school, parents must take responsibility to encourage a child's goal-setting and support the achievement of those goals. When a child has goals and the good guidance of parents and teachers, all things are possible, regardless of income, location, or race.

THE NEED FOR A WORK ETHIC

The basic religious covenant of earning your keep through honest work often falls on deaf ears today, and not without reason. We have lost a rigorous sense of a work ethic in our communities.

If a boy dreams of driving exotic and legendary sports cars, lunching at the Jockey Club in an Armani suit, and flying off to Paris for a night cap, he has a lot of work ahead of him. Fulfillment is likely to demand years and years of planning and right decisions, in addition to a great deal of education and achievement. Along the way, of course, priorities will likely rearrange themselves in his mind, and he may never enjoy such a "Hollywood day" as he dreamed about in his youth. Indeed, the man may decide to get a big, comfortable house in a quiet and friendly neighborhood where his daughter will grow up in safety. But no matter what career path he takes, he will need a powerful work ethic to help him achieve it.

The work ethic can be hard to come by. Often it fails to be developed because people cannot see the relationship between their grand goals and small, first-time jobs. But it is these jobs that develop one's work ethic. One learns habits of mind that will be essential at higher levels of education and employment.

And yet the work ethic has greater antagonists than those who cannot see how selling the newspaper is the first step on the road to fabulous fortune and fame. The disintegrating family structure and the welfare state are more forceful antagonists. The loss of religion and its ability to perform as a mediating structure can be blamed on the state's enthusiastic exercise of a strange deemphasis of religion and its secularist assault on the church and its services.

Greater than the problem of church and state, however, is the absence of traditional values in modern culture, which has also meant the absence of such wisdom as the work ethic. Many of the inner city's problems can be resolved by greater self-responsibility, self-determination, and economic initiative. Obviously, the way to rebuild the inner city, as well as rebuild the character of its citizens, is through a reaffirmation of a God-centered faith and the values which that faith prescribes and holds as true. Jewish, Christian, and Islamic communities seem to understand this point better than any governmental body or school board.

The old excuse that living in the ghetto or coming from a broken home is a severe disadvantage just does not hold water. Although over 50 percent of black children come from a single-parent household, this hardship does not absolve parents from their responsibilities to support, teach, and guide their children. It is true that a divorce can put extreme strain on familial relations and children, but that is a reason not to get divorced, and not to ask for more government money. Divorce is often made the excuse for educational underachievement for black children and their parents. The white divorce rate is nearly the same as the black rate, and yet it does not affect the education rate of white families as it does black families. All of the side effects of actions such as getting married, having children, getting an education, working or not working, and filing for divorce must be analyzed before the fact, not after the fact. These behaviors can be affected only by good, responsible parenting and solid traditional values.

In 1994 over 1.4 million black American households had incomes of $50,000 or more.[5] Why is it that we never hear complaints about divorce, lack of funding, and environment from this cross section of black America? Some of these people have gone to the same inner-city schools that the drug dealers have ravaged. The reasoning is simple: if you invest in yourself (get educated), the returns will be guaranteed, regardless of the economic status, supposed disadvantage, and social problems around you.

The urban black family needs to pull itself together and teach self-responsibility to its young adults. Those who are taught to own up to their responsibilities have a better chance to go farther and enjoy more successes than their dropout peers. In 1973 Frederick Harbison stated:

Human resources . . . constitute the ultimate basis for wealth of nations. Capital and natural resources are passive factors of production. Human resources, however, build social, economic, and political organizations—not to mention the development of the nation. Clearly, a country which is unable to develop the skills and knowledge of its people and to utilize them effectively in the national economy will be unable to develop anything else.[6]

Harbison's statement is macroeconomic, but it can be easily adapted to a microeconomic analysis. Inner-city residents will never develop to their full potential without a sound education.

Reverend Dr. Martin Luther King, Jr., had a dream. His dream was that all Americans would have the same opportunities and enjoy the same civil rights, and that their success would be measured by their achievements and not the color of their skin. It was a great dream, but it seems someone forgot to wake up the folks in the inner cities. It's kind of like the farmer who sows and cultivates the seeds, but then never harvests the fruits of his labor. The means to achieve greatness has been acquired, but the means has not been employed to get to the promised land. Black Americans can change that, and this change begins with a solid education and hard work.

NOTES

1. "Returns to Schooling" is the way economists describe the monetary rewards an education provides. See Marvin H. Kosters, "Be Cool, Stay in School," *The American Enterprise* (March/April 1990):60.

2. Michael P. Todano, *Economic Development in the Third World* (New York: Longman, 1989), 333.

3. *The American Almanac 1995–1996* (Austin, Tex.: Reference Press, 1995), 157.

4. Ibid., 469.

5. Ibid., 48.

6. Frederick H. Harbison, *Human Resources as the Wealth of Nations* (New York: Oxford University Press, 1973), 3.

10

THE ROLE OF BLACK CONSERVATIVE LEADERS IN THE 1990s

Gary Franks

The opponents of conservative welfare, crime, and education reform measures may well prevail even in the teeth of legislative decisions. . . . American government may lack the [practical] authority to require anything of black America without its leaders' specific consent. Progress may wait upon the emergence of a more conservative black leadership, willing to abandon the activists, reject racial liberalism, and enforce orthodox norms.

Lawrence Mead, political economist

The domestic conservative philosophy and its leaders have quite a job ahead of them, as domestic discussion and action head toward the issues of empowerment and responsibility.

It is often said that "black conservatism" is an oxymoron, and judging by our numbers, one could actually believe it. But black conservatism has a base in the American political landscape, and I believe there have been many misrepresentations of how blacks respond to the conservative message. If our numbers are small in high-profile positions, our opinions are more widely held than most pundits would have their readers believe.

On the key issues that are most important to black and white families, conservative arguments get a favorable hearing. When you ask black people if they should be allowed to have God in their lives, all would respond, "Yes."

So a moment of silence in our schools is not some hideous, off-base ritual. No one seeks to impose his religion or other beliefs on others. Because religion is a staple of black America, holding together the family and community, providing strength, and giving it initiative, this conservative message will be heard.

And what of our country, our duty to protect it and its most treasured symbols? if you would go up to a black person or family and ask: "Should we allow the flag to be desecrated, to be burned and walked upon? Is that something you get angry about?" An overwhelming majority would say: "Yes, that is not right. There are some symbols that are worth preserving and protecting."

And what of serving our country? There has been a lot of discussion about the racial makeup of our armed services. Some of the same people who fought to end the draft and instead have a volunteer army now want to bring back the draft and socially engineer our military. Well, we go up to our black person or family and say: "You have a choice available to you, to have a career where you are judged by your ability, where there is discipline and advancement and a safe retirement. But this career has its risks, yet it's your decision. Are you interested?" Many have said: "Yes, it is an honor and an opportunity to serve in the military." Our military is one of choice, and as someone who has four relatives in the military, I can tell you they are proud of their work and country.

MODEL OF RACIAL HARMONY

Many of our men and women who happen to be black have made a choice and are defending their country with great courage and intelligence. The former chairman of the Joint Chiefs of Staff is black, and black officers are leading men and women into combat. Is that so bad? It was not too long ago that blacks had to fight, just to fight. There was a time when the only place in which blacks could serve was a mess hall. And even when they were allowed to enlist, they were segregated and not recognized. So now the military has changed; it is a model of racial harmony, and it is a choice offered by the government to its people. This talk about how blacks who freely chose to join the military now do not belong there is insulting, and destroys the morale of all our military.

Now, are there reasons why the number of black enlistees is higher than the overall makeup of our country? Sure! When those men and women do return, whatever their color, they deserve the same consideration that all veterans enjoy. And government should offer more choices to blacks, and that occurs with empowerment. We have to approach old problems with new, results-oriented programs and solutions. Choices have to be tied to an improved economy as well as to an improved social order. These should be the building blocks for advancement. Black conservatives have to work harder to make their case, but when successful, they serve as a bridge to the many people who I believe are looking for new ways to get ahead or stay afloat.

STARTING WITH FAMILIES

And we have to start with our families. Talk of role models sounds old and tired, but it strikes at the heart of the problem. Many white students know what a certified accountant or an investment banker does and wish to enter those professions. Unfortunately, many black children do not have that type of goal in mind. When I was a younger man, those who took business courses were presumed to be looking to be secretaries, not bankers or insurance executives. We can make missiles that can fly down an alleyway and hit their targets. But many blacks lack the goals to strive for jobs that catapult them to a better life. Instead, they see the easy money of the street or the overblown salaries of rock stars and athletes, which only a few receive.

We offer more programs and disciplines than before, yet when one goes to fast-food restaurants, one sees cash registers whose punching keys are coded to products rather than to dollars and cents. Even recognition of numbers is not needed.

In short, we have to get our families, students, and teachers working for the same goals. Only when a family or an individual begins to believe and see they can make it will we break the cycle of dependence and begin to turn the corner. But what do we have now in many schools? We have violence in the school yards and classrooms. We have low scores, high dropout rates, and few role models. The traditional political course of more money, more task forces, and more studies will only perpetuate more endless poverty.

Black conservatives have to get involved and argue that a new approach is due, including support of private business and its efforts to improve the quality of schools. Government has been left behind in many respects. Corporations are frightened at the level of product that is coming into the workplace. While many large businesses have sufficient resources for special training, small to medium-sized businesses have tighter budgets. And unlike the fast-food chains that changed their cash registers, corporations are now working with schools to better prepare students for the real world.

Government must encourage more companies to participate, particularly in the inner urban areas, large and small. This will enable us to break up the monopoly of our present school systems, now held by many forces who cannot see the trees for the forest.

IMPORTANCE OF CHOICES

But this all gets back to giving choices to individuals. And when the supply is open to all, there are incentives and the product is delivered on time and in good working order. In Minnesota and East Harlem, New York, there have been successful stories of education through empowerment choices. Black conservatives can supplement this effort, and it should be the duty of black conservatives to bridge the gap of mistrust that does exist. But the bottom line is that if you pose these questions on choices for a secure education, most blacks, if not all, will say: "I agree. Something must be done."

It is up to conservatives to offer guidance and leadership. Conservatives have to show through actions that their philosophy is based on fairness. One rewards risk taking and initiative and allows those with little to use it to better their lot in life.

Small businesses are the backbone of our economy, and quite frankly, it will work to have government take a more constructive approach to improving the economic climate for medium to small companies. Small businesses can benefit from a successful empowerment program. If we strengthen the ability of business to find qualified candidates, then efficiency, new products, and expansion will result.

The number of businesses will grow, too. By building from small units of enterprise, our ability to be productive will rise and with it, the standards of living.

ATTAINING THE GOAL

Blacks and whites will see that when they are not limited to one frame of reference, a successful life is available through discipline, ambition, and the courage to take chances. All of us must work for a truly color-blind society, and conservatives—especially black ones—can help attain that goal with a more aggressive campaign to convince other black Americans that they can excel if they are presented with opportunities and choices.

NOTE

This essay is the edited transcript of Heritage Lecture #303 given February 7, 1991, at the Heritage Foundation in Washington, D.C.

III

PERSPECTIVES ON RACISM

The belief in white racism as the most basic problem confronting black Americans is the foundation of conventional black advocacy in this country. It is black conservatives' resistance to this cardinal doctrine that most infuriates and enrages their critics. In this section, the commitment to white racism is called into question. Is racism as prevalent as is commonly thought? Must blacks subscribe to the usual understanding of white racism in order to progress? Is white racism the only kind of racism in America?

In Chapter 11 of this section, Joseph G. Conti and Brad Stetson take an empirical look at the scope of white racism, in the form of a common-sense quiz. Chapter 12 presents Errol Smith's experience as a leading proponent of the highly controversial California ballot measure, which would eliminate state-administered racial and gender preferences, the California Civil Rights Initiative. Chapter 13 recounts Jesse Peterson's exploration of a Los Angeles ecumenical group's effort to elect more black politicians, as though this would somehow ensure black progress in the city. Chapter 14, by Marivic C. Francis, is a record of some typical reactions to Jesse Peterson's resistance to race-based black activism, and Deroy Murdock, in Chapter 15, reflects on the recent trend of predominantly minority trial juries rendering verdicts based on race rather than evidence.

While today there is an abundance of emoting and ambient arguments regarding racism, it is sadly rare for us to confine our dispute to objective grounds. This section as a whole is an attempt to help infuse the fractious discussion of racism in America with evidentially sound data and reasoning, an approach eminently characteristic of the black conservative voice.

11

ARE YOU REALLY A RACIST?
A COMMON-SENSE QUIZ

Joseph G. Conti and Brad Stetson

Race is a part of everything in America, you can't deny that!
Johnnie Cochran, Jr., millionaire

Recently, the host of a TV talk show told his breakfasting viewers that the "racism quiz" he was about to administer to them would reveal if they were "racists or liberals."

We can only hope that the absurdity of that false dichotomy troubled many viewers. Sadly, however, it may not have, for this assertion is only one in a long line of politically correct myths concerning race and racial politics that have been bathing the American public consciousness for decades.[1] These ideological fables significantly contribute to the wall of ignorance that prevents many political commentators and reporters from opening their minds to the unique point of view heard in the voice of the black conservative.

RACIAL HUMANISM

We believe there is a "spiral of silence" on racial issues: as the media-sanctioned voices of racial understanding have grown louder, expression of dissent—especially by blacks—has been inhibited.[2] The effect of this politically correct bullying is that many decent, fair-minded people of all colors are pressured into silence and are made to feel guilty for questioning the "official story" on race. Common-sense discussion about racial questions, especially in black communities of discourse, has suffered a *de facto* suppression. Along with it, a historically venerable position that we call "racial humanism"—a perspective best captured in Martin Luther King's call to judgment based on character, not color—has also suffered. It is to amplify the voice of racial humanism that we make these observations, in the form of a brief quiz.

1. *True or False, only whites can be racist.*

False. The truth of this idea is regularly taught as rock-solid fact in many forums, including elementary school classrooms, university lecture halls, church discussion groups, and MTV videos. "Only people in power can be racist," goes the reasoning, "and so only whites, the power-brokers, can be racists."[3] In stark contrast to this collectivist and deterministic thinking, racial humanism—as seen in the work of black dissidents who eschew race-consciousness and group identity—plainly asserts that anyone who hates on the basis of race is a racist. Reginald Denny, the truck driver beaten nearly to death during the 1992 Los Angeles riots, and the families of the people that Colin Ferguson murdered on a New York commuter train, know full well that African Americans—like all human beings—can be racists.[4]

Indeed, a main odium of misleading notions like "Only whites can be racist" is that they threaten to immunize a whole generation of minority youth from moral common sense and the confidence that their society is not set against them, a confidence they will need if they are to expend the needed effort to achieve their own social mobility. In *Shut up and Let the Lady Teach!*, journalist and teacher Emily Sachar illustrates this moral blindness with a story from her New York City school. Annoyed at the nomination of two Asians to be class leaders, a black youngster stood up in Sachar's classroom and announced, "No way I'm staying here if two slanty-eyed kids is [*sic*] running things." Sachar told him that he was free to run for the position too, but that he would have to refrain from racist remarks. The boy seemed truly shocked and replied softly, "That was a racist remark?" Jesse Peterson, a south central Los Angeles community activist who helps troubled black youth grow into mature men, believes that racism among black teens is one of the most tragic, underreported stories in America today. Peterson told us, "A black gang member told us during a meeting, that he refuses to learn from a teacher at school—because the man is white. He said, 'I hate all white people.' Many black kids think this way, and they don't even understand how they're hurting themselves."[5]

Those who deny that the evil of racism comes in all colors are blind to an important truth, a truth that was best expressed by Martin Luther King, Jr.: "It is not a sign of weakness, but a sign of high maturity to rise to a level of self-criticism." We call all Americans to answer this challenge and to stand guard against the balkanizing demons of ethnic chauvinism and racism, whatever color their mask.

Perhaps the hardest thing in life is to love the stranger. We are all given to be wary of those who are different from us, whether those differences be religious, cultural, or racial. Yet, it is undeniably a necessary prerequisite for any just society that we judge other people not by their exterior, but by their interior. This is the heart of the racial humanism that a balkanized America needs to embrace. We wholeheartedly affirm this ethical imperative and recommend it anew to our rending national fabric. Judging someone based solely on the content of her character must become not merely a platitude, but a widely practiced principle of social order and policy. We must know each other as we actually are and interact on that basis alone, not according to how we imagine one another to be.

It has become painfully apparent that one of the greatest hindrances to fostering this racial humanism is human nature itself. James Madison put it well in *The Federalist*, no. 51, when he said "If men were angels, no government would be necessary."[6] Human beings are capable of great and redemptive acts, but the record of history makes it undeniable that we are also capable of great evil. Racism is one of those evils. But for the sake of our commonweal, we must understand that racism is a function of human nature. It is an individual shortcoming, and everyone—whatever their ethnicity or class— is capable of it. In this country today what would be civicly restorative would be an end to ethnic chauvinism—on the part of all Americans—and for a return to the common-sense knowledge that unless each of us guards his or her own heart and mind, we too could enter into the poisoned quicksand of racial animosity, which accomplishes nothing but the rending of our nation, and it only feeds the ugly part of human nature.

2. *True or false, "institutional racism" so permeates American society that it hardly matters if African Americans and other minorities try to succeed, since the effects of discrimination inevitably shut them out of the job market.*

False. Recently, the millionaire "rapper" Chuck D.—one of the most influential voices in black youth culture—spoke to a *Spin* magazine interviewer about the uselessness of a college education for blacks: "I can go to college and high school and get top grades, and when I go out into the job market, I don't know anything about business, which means business is a family thing, you understand what I am saying? If you ain't got family, you're not going to get that fuckin' job."[7]

Chuck D. is not the only one to beat the drum of futility in this way; speeches by many mainstream minority leaders commonly sound the same theme. But are they right? To find out, we turn to recent statistics from the U.S. Department of Labor which reveal the relationship between black educational attainment and black employment. For every significant level of increase in education realized by twenty-five- to thirty-four-year-old blacks, the percent of black unemployment drops by one-half. This means that blacks with a four-year college degree are roughly six times as likely to be employed than those who only have a high school diploma. Is this really surprising?

Another millionaire rapper called "Ice Cube" says: "The American Dream is not for Blacks. Blacks who [still believe in that dream] are kidding themselves. There's only room in that dream for a few Blacks."[8] Once again, the facts contradict the rap. Ice Cube is predictably unaware that black college-educated females, on average, currently earn 125 percent of what white college-educated females earn, according to syndicated columnist and economist Walter Williams of George Mason University.[9] Chuck D. and Ice Cube are just two of the unreflective voices in popular culture who unthinkingly parrot the civil rights establishment's "official story" of America as an inveterately racist country, with systematic racial discrimination literally everywhere. As New York writer Jim Sleeper put it, many people today are committed to seeing "racism in every leaf that falls."[10]

Despite this quasireligious commitment, scholarly studies show that an overwhelming majority of white Americans now reject racism as evil and that the racial attitudes of whites *have* changed for the better over the last thirty-five years. For example, social researchers Paul M. Sniderman and Thomas Piazza report in their book *The Scar of Race* that today blacks are more likely than whites to hold negative stereotypes about blacks.[11] Yet the mantras of "racist America" drone on, perhaps best exemplified in the words of the new prince of race-baiting—himself a multimillionaire who recently signed one of the richest nonfiction book deals in American history—attorney Johnnie Cochran, Jr., who famously chanted during the O. J. Simpson murder trial, "Race is a part of everything in America."

But while the superstars of race-hustling and the liberal voices of higher education and the mainstream media continue to mechanically repeat the script about "racism in America," there is apparent now a different picture clearly showing that they are simply presenting a false and inaccurate verdict on the state of social life in the United States. At any rate, if racism is the impenetrable barrier to black progress they claim it is, one would expect all blacks to be affected by it equally, but they clearly are not. We all know that some blacks succeed and others fail, just as some whites and Hispanics succeed, and others fail. Carefully consider the following resume of facts about black achievement in American society, routinely eclipsed by headline-grabbing racialist rhetoric:

- While 30.7 percent of America's 30 million blacks have incomes below the poverty line—despite billions of dollars spent on welfare programs—the population of middle-class and affluent blacks has been dramatically expanding. Today two-thirds of all American blacks earn at least a middle-class income. "You've got one segment moving up, and the other stuck at the bottom," says William O'Hare, a social demographer at the University of Louisville. Of those moving up, nearly one in seven black families had an annual income of $50,000 or more in 1989, according to O'Hare's study of black income, compared with only one in seventeen in 1967.[12]

- Blacks earning $50,000 a year or more are the fastest growing income group in America.[13]

- The *Los Angeles Times* reports that since the 1960s, the percentage of affluent black Americans has more than doubled.[14]

- Economist Thomas Sowell notes in *The Economics and Politics of Race* that by the late 1960s, black males from families with a library card, magazines, and other literature in the home reached high-level occupations as often as white males of similar backgrounds.[15]

- Again according to Thomas Sowell, in families where both parents are college educated and both parents work, black families make more than white families. This is the case in all parts of the United States, for families of all ages.[16]

- According to *Time* magazine, from 1982 to 1987, the number of companies owned by blacks increased by a third, and their gross incomes more than doubled. During this same period, nonblack-owned businesses increased by only 14 percent.[17]

- During the period 1973–1994, the current-dollar revenues of the top 100 black-owned industrial firms—as listed by *Black Enterprise* magazine—increased from $473 million to $6.7 billion.[18]

- The richest American singer (Whitney Houston) is black, the richest American comedian (Bill Cosby) is black, the richest American entertainer (Oprah Winfrey) is black, and the richest American athlete (Michael Jordan) is black. The two Americans given the high honor of lighting the Olympic torches the last two times the Olympic games were held in this country were both black—Rafer Johnson and Muhammad Ali.

• In recent nationwide political popularity polls, Colin Powell—who is black— handily defeated President Bill Clinton. These same polls also showed more whites than blacks supported Powell.

This hardly sounds like the profile of a systemically racist, anti-black nation.[19] A personal observation by Shelby Steele, author of *The Content of Our Character*, echoes this conclusion and its implication in a simple way: "For every white I have met who is a racist, I have met twenty more who have seen me as an equal. And of those twenty, ten have wished me only the best as an individual. This . . . has been my actual reality. I believe it is time for blacks to begin the shift from a wartime to a peacetime identity, from fighting for opportunity to the seizing of it."[20] None of this is to say that racism is totally dead and gone, but rather, that thoughtful, sensitive dialogue—the kind engendered by racial humanism—requires that civil discourse be based on the facts, even when those facts testify to the institutional and social weakness of racism.

3. *True or false, when welfare critics talk about straightening out the welfare system, they are secretly expressing racist attitudes toward poor minorities.*

False. This is a favorite of media pundits, who commonly dismiss public calls for welfare reform as "playing the race card." For instance, one television commentator blamed the 1992 Los Angeles riots not on the looters and arsonists who sacked the city, but on those who "fanned these flames with codewords about 'welfare queens,' 'equal opportunity,' and 'quotas.' " His unstated message was plain: "If you criticize welfare programs, or expect certain behavior from those on welfare, you are a racist."

This "decoding" breeds a social silence on the issue of welfare. This silence—the refusal to voice unpopular but heartfelt opinions—ends up being most damaging to the black poor, according to black neighborhood activist Robert Woodson. Sharply criticizing the welfare system, Woodson and other critics believe that the black community must free itself from the welfare professionals whose primary mission has become the maintenance of clients. He argues that this "poverty pentagon" literally rides on the backs of the black poor, with nearly 75 percent of monies intended for the poor going instead to the bureaucratic apparatus—that is, to the "helpers" of the poor.

The black family has been especially hard hit by the welfare system. With few exceptions, for a mother to qualify for the largest welfare program, Aid to Families with Dependent Children (AFDC), she *must* be unmarried. This policy has set into motion a tragic set of social dynamics. In Detroit's nearly all-black school district of 170,000 students, some 70 percent of them are being raised by single mothers—and nearly two out of three boys entering high school in Detroit do not graduate.[21] Now, it is important to stress that there is nothing intrinsically "racial" about these dynamics. For example, more than half the children born in Sweden—with its hefty welfare packages—are the result of unwed pregnancies.[22] The point is that welfarism contributes to family dissolution and ultimately hurts the people involved with it.[23] Liberal *ad hominems* aside, this is the motivation of welfare critics. Welfare programs and policies are a classic case of the iatrogenic nature of activist government policy: intending to help, it hurts.[24] Indeed, social scientist George Gilder has gone as far as to point to the Welfare State and its effects as *the chief* cause of black poverty.[25]

4. True or false, statistical disparities between whites and minorities are indicative of racism.

False. Statistical disparities *do* exist between black and whites in many areas, but do they *necessarily* indicate racial prejudice? Under the contemporary regime of "proportionalism," in many venues, from education to government contracts to the professions, all that is necessary to establish a presumption of discrimination and unfairness is to show that women and minorities are not distributed in a given area in exact proportion to their distribution in the population. This is a profoundly simplistic view of human accomplishment and free choice.[26] Thomas Sowell has coined a term—*the civil rights vision*—to describe this outlook, which automatically accounts for various differences of status and income by charging "racism." When the civil rights vision automatically identifies racial discrimination as the root cause of income differences, it ignores other critical factors, says Sowell. For example, while it is a fact that black Ph.D.s earn less, on the average, than white Ph.D.s, it is important to know that the economic value of a degree is related to its field of expertise, as some fields pay more than others. As it happens, a great percentage of African Americans have taken Ph.D.s in education—not a very lucrative field, relatively speaking. Had they taken Ph.D.s in fields common to nonblacks (e.g., engineering, computer science, mathematics), this "conclusive" evidence for racism would evaporate.[27] Often social and cultural factors—apart from discrimination—can explain statistical differences. Of course, the same is true for differentials in the earnings of men and women. For example, male physicians generally outearn female physicians,[28] because (a) they tend to go into more lucrative specialties, and (b) they work longer hours than female physicians, who often elect to work fewer hours in exchange for spending time with their children.

Again, ethnic discrepancies in income—when viewed through the prism of victimhood that is the tired civil rights vision—invariably link black poverty to racism. But this perspective ignores the crucial relationship of social mobility to individual differences. For instance, according to a 1986 study, young black women who graduate from high school (and avoid unwed pregnancy) have better than a 90 percent chance of living above the poverty line.[29] The poverty rate for those who either don't graduate high school or have an unwed pregnancy in their teen years is dramatically higher. This disparity can be attributed to individual differences in behavior rather than racism. Indeed, for married couples outside the South, black family income was 78 percent of white in 1959, 91 percent in 1969, and 96 percent in 1970. But black female-headed families have had declining real incomes during a period when black husband-wife families have had rising real incomes, both absolutely and relative to white families. Personal behavioral choices most plausibly account for such trends.

The forces of the market are not race-conscious. The distribution of income in the professions—from physician down to schoolteacher—is what it is regardless of the race of the practitioner. In 1996 America, the rewards of education, technical knowledge, experience, discipline, and diligence accrue to those who have invested themselves, not to those whose skin tones match the line on a color bar long since cut down by a national conscience stirred with a vision of colorblindness.

5. *True or false, only persons of a certain race or ethnicity ought to speak about issues related to that race or ethnicity.*

False. "IT'S A BLACK THING, YOU WOULDN'T UNDERSTAND." Maybe you have seen this T-shirt motto. If we take its message at face value, it calls into question the possibility of participatory democracy itself, as it implies that only blacks can deliberate and comment on issues affecting blacks. But the fact is that in our pluralistic society, there is no such thing as a social issue that affects only one sector of the population. No group exists in a social vacuum, completely isolated from all others. Our destinies, as individuals and as members of a common society, are tightly intertwined.

Thus, it is impossible for a white American to cast a ballot that does not somehow affect a black or Hispanic American, and vice versa. And so it goes for all racial and ethnic groups. We are obligated, then, to mutually reflect on the full range of social issues, including those that uniquely affect other races. Such reflection naturally results in the expression of a variety of perspectives on racial issues, and this drives us to a clear understanding of the radical uniqueness of persons, not as racial beings but as human beings. In turn, this understanding has a humanizing effect on culture, reminding us that we must extend respect and goodwill to cognitive as well as ethnic minorities. This is the meaning of racial humanism, and it is the precondition of a social discourse that aims at genuine liberty for all.

Opposing this perspective is the color-coordinated thinking that is so rife in American politics today. This deterministic posture—blacks think one way, whites another—is counter to the very nature of democracy itself, wherein persons of all backgrounds are supposed to reflectively cooperate in common government for common ends. This is the kind of government that, in Lincoln's words, is "of the people, by the people, and for the people." But it's not hard to see how maintaining the myth of color-coordinated thinking serves the ends of the many "rights" and advocacy groups.[30] If all blacks think alike, then the civil rights groups become the arbiters of "the black experience" and the unchallenged representatives of every single black person. This magnifies their power. Similarly, Hispanic rights groups deploy the fiction of "La Raza," as though Cubans, Mexicans, Puerto Ricans, Guatemalans, and Salvadorans had some strong common ethnic experience. In this way, these lobbies maximize their political capital and social influence, strengthening their ability to intimidate media and press claims against institutions.

In contrast to the counterintuitive world of color-coordinated thinking, black conservatives insist with Dr. King that people be judged on inward qualities, not outward ones. This common-sense standard of fairness presupposes our ability to understand and evaluate the social situation and morality of all people, however different they are from us in appearance. Indeed, the very logic of the original civil rights movement operated under the assumption that whites and others could understand the plight of discrimination and repression facing blacks, and move to provide appropriate redress. Of course, then, redress meant equality under the law. Today calls for social justice have been revised to require special preference, race-based entitlement and equality of outcomes. In effect, it insists on discrimination in the other direction. This is one of the cardinal ironies of our day, routinely ignored by reporters, editors, and academics loath to incur the wrath of the race lobby.

Interestingly, the sensible idea that we can understand persons different from ourselves is still in use by the left today, but only when it suits their ends, for example, in "multicultural" education. Multiculturalism as a philosophy of education presumes that we can understand—and benefit from—

cultures and human experiences much different from our own, no matter what our own heritage is. Surely this sweeping understanding embraces differences far deeper than simply skin color. Hence, according to the very logic of multiculturalism, it should be possible for whites to speak about problems and hardships facing blacks and black progress, just as many black critics have spoken so eloquently about the immorality of Jim Crow and the racist attitudes held for so long by many white Americans. But unfortunately, we rarely if ever hear public acknowledgment of this possibility.

In a radically pluralistic society like ours, everyone's interests are perforce united. Thus, there is a need—out of both self-interest and fellow concern—to reflect on the social context and personal character of our neighbors. This should be done with thoughtfulness and sensitivity, along with a rigorous honesty. We must not deny our full humanity, for the sake of political advantage or political correctness, and pretend that our minds cannot cross the artificial boundaries of race, class, and gender.[31]

The United States, at the end of the American century, is at a racial crossroads. We can continue down the jarring path of group identification, with its wounding rhetoric and inherent hostility, or we can turn toward racial humanism, with its individualist ethic and emphasis on personal responsibility. We urge the latter course, in the hopes of the widespread recognition of the simple truth that regrettably few pluralistic cultures ever comprehend and that our race-conscious public life is today so far from: we are more alike than we are different, more human than we are racial.

NOTES

1. One recent example is United States Senator Bill Bradley's assertion that "To say that someone who opposes affirmative action is racist denies the possibility that the person may just be ignorant" (Bill Bradley, "Ending Racism Can Never Be Just about Numbers," *Los Angeles Times*, 15 January 1996, B9). In other words, reasoned, principled dissent about the value and wisdom of affirmative action is impossible. Either one supports affirmative action, or needs to be educated into support for affirmative action, or is simply a racist.

2. For explanation of the psychological and sociological dynamics of the spiral of silence, and how it operates in various contexts, see Elizabeth Noelle-Neumann, "The Spiral of Silence: A Theory of Public Opinion," *Journal of Communication* 24 (spring 1974): 43–51; and Noelle-Neumann, *The Spiral of Silence* (Chicago: University of Chicago Press, 1984). See also Timur Kuran, "Private and Public Preferences," *Economics and Philosophy* 6 (1990): 1–26; Frederick R. Lynch, *Invisible Victims: White Males and the Crisis of Affirmative Action* (New York: Praeger

Publishers, 1991) and Joseph G. Conti and Brad Stetson, *Challenging the Civil Rights Establishment* (Westport, Conn.: Praeger Publishers, 1993).

3. For a general description of this perspective, see John Black, "Can a Black Person Be a Racist?" *Atlanta Journal and Constitution*, 20 February 1994, P1.

4. For a discussion of black racism, see David Horowitz, "Identifying Black Racism: The Last Taboo," *Orange County Register*, 10 December 1995, Commentary 3. For a comprehensive look at this question, see Dinesh D'Souza's chapter "Bigotry in Black and White: Can African Americans Be Racist?" in his book *The End of Racism* (New York: Free Press, 1995), 387–429. See also Jared Taylor, *Paved with Good Intentions* (New York: Carrol and Graf, 1992), 64–73, 233–240, 256–260.

5. Brad Stetson and Joseph G. Conti, interview with Jesse Peterson, December 4, 1995.

6. James Madison, "The Federalist No. 51," in *The Federalist*, edited by Jacob E. Cooke (Middletown, Conn.: Wesleyan University Press, 1961), 349.

7. Chuck D., interviewed by Vivien Goldman, *Spin*, October 1992, 46.

8. A. S. Doc Young, "Negatives and Positives," *Los Angeles Sentinel*, 14 November 1991.

9. See *Social Science and Modern Society* (January/February 1993): 85.

10. For Jim Sleeper's perspective on race in America, see his excellent meditation, *The Closest of Strangers* (New York: W. W. Norton, 1990).

11. See Paul M. Sniderman and Thomas Piazza, *The Scar of Race* (Cambridge, Mass.: Harvard University Press, 1993), 45.

12. See "Gap Grows Between Black Middle Class and Those Mired in Poverty, Study Finds," *Los Angeles Times*, 9 August 1991, A27.

13. Cited in Robert L. Woodson, "The New Politics in Action," in "Left and Right: The Emergence of a New Politics in the 1990s?", a conference sponsored by the Heritage Foundation and the Progressive Foundation, Washington, D.C., 30 October 1991, 47.

14. "Gap Grows between Black Middle Class and Those Mired in Poverty, Study Finds," A27.

15. Thomas Sowell, *The Economics and Politics of Race* (New York: William Morrow, 1983), 194.

16. Thomas Sowell, *Civil Rights: Rhetoric or Reality?* (New York: William Morrow, 1984), 80–81. For a thoughtful examination of the dynamics affecting average group income and the subtleties of measuring group income statistically, see Sowell's book *The Vision of the Annointed: Self Congratulation as a Basis for Social Policy* (New York: Basic Books, 1995), 31–63. For an extended analysis of the relationship between race and culture in economic, political, and social contexts, see Sowell's *Race and Culture: A Worldview* (New York: Basic Books, 1994).

17. See *Time*, 13 March 1989, 58–68.

18. George Gilder, "The Roots of Black Poverty," *Wall Street Journal*, 30 October 1995, A18.

19. For discussion of the social and political implications of this profile, see David

Horowitz, "Denzel, Dennis and Shaq Belie the 'Color Bar,' " *Los Angeles Times*, 23 July 1996, B7.

20. Shelby Steele, *The Content of Our Character: A New Vision of Race in America* (New York: St. Martin's Press, 1990), 175.

21. *New York Times*, 14 August 1991, A11.

22. Thomas Sowell, "Throwing Money and Intercepting It," *Washington Times*, 19 February 1991.

23. For a comprehensive examination of the social corrosiveness of fatherlessness—one of the major social contributions of the Welfare State—see the excellent study by David Blankenhorn, *Fatherless America: Confronting Our Most Urgent Social Problem* (New York: Basic Books, 1995).

24. For an excellent study of the harmfulness of current welfare policy, see Lawrence Mead, *Beyond Entitlement* (New York: Macmillan, 1986); and Mead, *The New Politics of Poverty* (New York: Basic Books, 1992), especially 185–209.

25. Gilder, "The Roots of Black Poverty."

26. For an excellent study of why individuals from different groups are not distributed in exact proportion to their representation in the general population, see Lawrence Harrison, *Who Prospers? How Cultural Values Shape Economic and Political Success* (New York: Basic Books, 1992). For an analysis and refutation of the egalitarianism that underlies "proportionalism" and rhetoric about "underrepresentation," see Aaron Wildavsky, *The Rise of Radical Egalitarianism* (Washington, D.C.: American University Press, 1991), and William A. Henry III, *In Defense of Elitism* (New York: Doubleday, 1994). Some recent political analysis has suggested that egalitarianism in public policy is, today, an inevitable electoral "dead-end," and those who are inclined to advocate liberal social principles and politics should revise their programs accordingly. See Mickey Kaus, *The End of Equality* (New York: Basic Books, 1992).

27. Sowell, *The Economics and Politics of Race*, 140. See also D'Souza, *The End of Racism*, 304. D'Souza points out that in 1992 nearly one-half of all black doctorates were in education, with most of the rest in sociology and social work.

28. "The Male Gynecologist: Soon to Be Extinct?" *Wall Street Journal*, 7 February 1996, B1. See also "Female Doctor's Pay Catches Up to Men's—If Hours Are Same," *Orange County Register*, 11 April 1996, News 7.

29. William Bennett, *The De-Valuing of America* (New York: Summit Books, 1992), 197.

30. For a discussion of the degeneration of American political discourse into "rights talk," and the activistic social and political role of rights groups, see Mary Ann Glendon, *Rights Talk* (New York: Free Press, 1991).

31. For a case study of color-coordinated thinking, see Brad Stetson, "Ideas Have No Color," *Social Justice Review* 86 (January/February 1995): 23–24.

12

MY EXPERIENCE WITH THE CALIFORNIA CIVIL RIGHTS INITIATIVE

Errol Smith

The State shall not discriminate against, or grant preferential treatment to, any individual or group on the basis of race, sex, color, ethnicity, or national origin in the operation of public employment, public education or public contracting.
California Civil Rights Initiative, operative clause

Nothing, not all the armies in the world, can stop an idea whose time has come.
Victor Hugo

In 1994 I joined the advisory board of the California Civil Rights Initiative (CCRI). The board was formed to develop a strategy that would bring to an end the use of racial and gender preferences in public contracting, public education, and public employment. Before the initiative had even qualified to be placed on the ballot in California, it effectively plunged the country into a national debate on affirmative action.[1] It also led to a spate of court decisions, legislative and administrative actions that profoundly changed the character of affirmative action in America.

As vice-chair and senior spokesman for the initiative, I traveled the country debating the merits of eliminating the use of racial and gender preferences. Inevitably, I encountered the same question: "Why would someone like you be in support of an initiative that would end affirmative action?" Of course this was code language for "Why would a black man be part of a campaign to end programs designed primarily to benefit blacks?"

Discrimination Is Always Wrong

I routinely responded by quoting Dr. Martin Luther King, Jr., who said in one of his most arresting speeches that even if his Jewish brothers and sisters told him they didn't need his help to fight bigotry toward Jews, he would still "take a stand against anti-Semitism because it's wrong, it's unjust and it's evil." Similarly, I have chosen to take a stand against our nation's current racial policies because I believe they are profoundly wrong, significantly unjust, and inherently evil.

Is it right to require Chinese applicants to an elite high school in San Francisco to score ten points higher than blacks on entrance exams to qualify for admission? Is it just that white males in certain occupations are precluded from even competing for opportunities because their skin's melanin content roughly approximates that of those who once discriminated against blacks? Is it fair to deem the son of an affluent black family disadvantaged because so many other blacks live in poverty—while declaring a poor young white male privileged because he looks a lot like the CEO of the nearest Fortune 500 firm? Isn't the notion of creating social policy based on skin color the very evil Dr. King gave his life to end? *The benign intentions and lofty ideals that gave birth to affirmative action have, in a perverse twist of executive orders and legal interpretations, betrayed the intent and the spirit of King's dream.*

But beyond the lofty principles of social rectitude lie more pragmatic considerations. Perhaps the most important of these is the perception that affirmative action is synonymous with lowering standards. Tales of "race-normed" test scores, waived minimum standards to meet *de facto* racial quotas, and substandard performance have become part of the lore of affirmative action. This perception has engendered a climate that has far-reaching ramifications for minorities in general, and blacks in particular. As a black American, it makes little difference what Ivy League university you attend, what degrees you attain, or what academic accomplishments you achieve. What even the most talented black will encounter, as he or she enters the marketplace is a lingering presumption of inferiority, an abiding suspicion about his or her competence.

This phenomenon is due, at least in part, to the fact that for years civil rights elites have argued that without preferences, special programs, and double standards, blacks, women, and selected other minorities cannot compete in the marketplace. This argument is premised on the idea that blacks in particular are so bereft of resources, innovation, and the fundamentals to adapt that there is no hope, no salvation, and no life for black Americans beyond preferences.

PERCEPTIONS

The result of this argument has been a further entrenching of the perception of black inferiority, and the ramifications of this lingering perception have been far-reaching. Perhaps the most dramatic effect is that we have now caused an entire generation of black Americans—though they are part of a group that earns in the aggregate over $400 billion annually and who according to George Fraser's book *Success Runs in Our Race* have over $5 billion in intellectual capital—to doubt themselves and their abilities. So even though this generation of blacks is the freest and most affluent people of African descent in the history of civilization, they have come to believe that without special programs they cannot succeed. This is a tragedy of immeasurable proportions and an insult to the legacy of earlier generations of black Americans who strove to open doors of opportunity for black people today.

The most corrosive, debilitating, undermining, handicapping, destructive remnant of slavery and segregation is the perception of black inferiority. Daily, the purveyors of self-esteem argue that the stigma of black inferiority is an insidious legacy of this nation's racial history. It follows then, that any racial policy that reinforces this stigma should be viewed with suspicion, if not contempt. Moreover, it is doubtful that any genuine respect or perception of equality between blacks and whites can ever be attained in the presence of social policies that deemphasize merit and seek to force acceptance of double standards.

In my view, the debate over racial and gender preferences comes down to just two critically important questions. First, "What kind of nation do we want to create?" And second, "What kind of nation are we actually creating?" Are our nation's social policies ultimately moving us toward a country that will one day fulfill Dr. King's dream, or are we sinking deeper into the morass of racial enmity, balkanization, and gender and color-coded opportunity?

Supreme Court Associate Justice Sandra Day O'Connor wrote that at the heart of our Constitution's guarantee of equal protection is the simple command that all Americans be treated as individuals and not components of racial, ethnic, religious, or national class. Conversely, our nation's current racial policies are premised on the notion that we are members of groups first and individuals second. This, in my mind, is not only unconstitutional but fundamentally un-American.

In the landmark Supreme Court case *Brown v. Board of Education,* Associate Justice Thurgood Marshall wrote that legal distinctions based on race or ancestry are odious and invidious. Marshall was right in 1964, and his words are still right today. The only remaining question now is how many other black Americans will rise up and defend the immutable rightness of the principles on which the civil rights movement was originally built.

NOTE

1. For a general flavor of the growing national discontent over affirmative action around the time of the California Civil Rights Initiative's drive for ballot qualification, see the following representative articles: Irving Kristol, "The Tragic Error of Affirmative Action," *Wall Street Journal,* 1 August 1994; Errol Smith, "An Initiative That Can Accomplish King's Dream," *Los Angeles Times,* 23 January 1995, B9; Craig Daniel Turk, "How Democrats May Dodge Certain Defeat," *Los Angeles Times,* 26 February 1995, M6; Joanne Jacobs, "The Affirmative Action Sex Ruse Won't Work," *Orange County Register,* 15 March 1995, Metro 8; "Whites' Affirmative Action Outcry Gets Louder," *Orange County Register,* 12 November 1995, News 14; K. L. Billingsly, "Student Revolt on Affirmative Action," *Wall Street Journal,* 12 October 1995, A22; Walter Williams, "Affirmative Action: Why Can't More Blacks Qualify for Universities," *Orange County Register,* 26 July 1995, Metro 7; "Connerly: 'Man with a Mission'," *Orange County Register,* 23 January 1996, News 14; Ward Connerly, "An Ugly Campaign to Preserve Quotas," *Wall Street Journal,* 25 September 1996, A22.

For a helpful general discussion of the social corrosiveness of affirmative action policies, see Paul Craig Roberts and Lawrence M. Stratton, *The New Color Line: How Quotas and Privilege Destroy Democracy* (Washington, D.C.: Regnery Publishing, 1995), and Frederick Lynch, *Invisible Victims: White Males and the Crisis of Affirmative Action* (New York: Praeger, 1991). See also the seminal works by Nathan Glazer, *Affirmative Discrimination: Ethnic Inequality and Public Policy* (New York: Basic Books, 1975), and Thomas Sowell, *Preferential Policies* (New York: William Morrow, 1990).

13

RACE CONFAB: AN EXERCISE IN FUTILITY

Jesse Peterson

During 1970 and 1971 angry black leaders were in demand on the lecture circuit. [One of them] traveled to Detroit and Baltimore to display his rage to admiring audiences.

Scott C. Davis, writer

A long-standing and useless practice of urban black America is the emphasis on politicians and the political as a means to black progress. Often this emphasis takes the form of striving to elect blacks to political office, especially high office.

RACE RALLY

On Saturday, April 1, 1995, the Los Angeles Ecumenical Congress continued this dubious tradition by holding a "Mayor's Race '97 Confab." The Los Angeles Ecumenical Congress is a group of liberal black ministers and community power brokers who periodically meet to further their cause, and for some reason they thought that I, as a leader of a community group, Brotherhood Organization of a New Destiny (BOND), would be their ally. At any rate, having been invited, I attended.

The speakers all represented one point of view—leftist—and they were all black. So much for diversity. The tirades delivered were all predictable: The contract with America is only a contract with whites, not blacks; the Republican party is trying to turn back the clock on black progress; the Los Angeles city power structure is deliberately trying to keep blacks out of office; blacks must stick together and vie for the same political goals; all black citizens must support black candidates, and so on.

Listening to them speak, I was struck with the idea that each one was effectively instilling fear, anger, and even hatred into the minds of each audience member. In my view this was an attempt at control. I see this frequently among black community leaders all across the country. Their rhetoric of suspicion and anger works to their own benefit, because it subtly says to the black community, "I'm your only hope; black politicians and organizations are our only hope."

BITTERNESS

I heard from these speakers only resentment and fear. They imparted no sense of love or gratitude for this country, and no encouragement for black youth. There was no racial outreach, no intention of furthering racial harmony among blacks and nonblacks. Most of all, no spirit of forgiveness was apparent. Of course this is ironic, since most of the speakers were ministers and preachers of various kinds. The message they brought was not forward-looking; it was completely rooted in the past, in the wrongs of the past, and in how angry we should be about it today.

The entire depressing experience reminded me of my youth, and how the words of liberal black leaders made me seethe with rage and hatred toward whites and America itself. I think that line of speech harmed me as a youth, and I think that black youth today who hear it are also harmed. They are discouraged and angered, not at all inspired to cooperate with the American social, economic, and educational mainstream. This manner of speech is very common in political black America, but it is rarely reported honestly by reporters and media, who are generally too cowardly to portray black power brokers in an unflattering way, even if that would be the most honest portrayal. In the case of this meeting, however, no media of any kind were present.

As this sad group of speeches came to an end, it came time for questions and answers. The organizers of this meeting were reluctant to allow people to ask their questions themselves, instead preferring they all be written down, so that they could be edited. After I insisted I be allowed to speak, however,

I was reluctantly allowed to do so. I stood up and said, "Why is it that every speaker here spoke about how bad white people are, but nobody spoke about the decline of morals in many black communities?"

They were not pleased. Speakers looked at each other, audience members shifted uncomfortably in their seats, and the moderator quickly began reading Bible verses, then called the meeting to a close. During the closing prayer, the minister who was saying the prayer indirectly called me names, "troublemaker" and the like. I was identified with the enemies of God and was called to repentance, all for the good of black America. These none too subtle condemnations of me were greeted with shouts of "Amen!," "That's right!" and "Go ahead!"

As everyone filed out of the church where the meeting was held, the bright Los Angeles sun hit our eyes. I thought about how long it would take for the light of the truth about black progress—that it comes through personal responsibility, not political action—to dawn on these community giants, these merchants of race and resentment.

14

RACIAL RAGE: THE RESPONSE
TO JESSE PETERSON

Marivic C. Francis

If I had a gun, I'd kill you.
> A nationally prominent black minister, whispering to Jesse Peterson
> during an intermission in their debate.

As the public relations director for Brotherhood Organization of a New Destiny (BOND), I have seen at firsthand the furious rage Jesse Peterson's message provokes in black audiences. His bluntness and unwillingness to cater to the conventions of political debate at first shocks and then enrages many listeners. But in my opinion there is much to learn from this common response.

"YOU CAN'T TALK ABOUT BLACK PEOPLE THAT WAY!"

Perhaps one of the most dramatic examples of race-based anger at Jesse Peterson followed his appearance on an ABC News "Nightline" Town Hall Meeting. The show was assembled to discuss the verdict in the O. J. Simpson murder case, and ways of defusing the racial tension in Los Angeles and the nation that had resulted. When it was Jesse's chance to speak, he said he was unsurprised by the verdict, because he knew that a majority black jury would not convict a wealthy and famous black man accused of killing a white woman. He explained that the desire for revenge for past injustices that has been drilled into the black public by black politicians and civil rights "leaders" has created a mindset that will excuse wrongs for the sake of making up for past injustices. The high-profile Simpson case was a chance for black America to repay white America for slavery and Jim Crow, and the prevailing moral posture of black America justified doing that.

The audience of L.A. racial power brokers was enraged. The first man to the microphone after Jesse turned to him and said that O. J. Simpson was obviously innocent, and that justice had been done. He then raised his voice, and decried Jesse's "white mind," and wondered aloud how it was that a black man had come to think like a white person. After the show—which was a useless forum overwhelmed by liberal nostrums—several young black men in attendance surrounded Jesse and blatantly threatened to kill him. "You can't talk about black people that way," one of them said. Jesse gave the man a business card and invited him to a BOND meeting. They grumbled some expletives and sauntered away. This whole debacle reminded me of the time when Jesse spoke at a multiracial Los Angeles community forum, denouncing pathologies like out-of-wedlock birth, crime, and rage in black neighborhoods. After he spoke, a black woman approached him. She looked troubled, and said to him, her voice trembling with emotion, "I agreed with everything you said about our problems, but you don't say that stuff about black people in front of white people, you just can't say those kinds of things." Jesse told her what he always tells people who say that: truth is more important than race, and black people who live in troubled areas need to stand against the crime and self-destructive behavior that is ruining their neighborhoods, and not try to hide dysfunction. Self-criticism is a virtue, not a vice. Black liberals and conventional black advocates are unwilling to understand this.

Jesse's public comments criticizing the hate-politics of Louis Farrakhan and his self-aggrandizing Million Man March have received a similar reaction. Jesse said that the march did nothing to help black people, its symbolism serving only to legitimize Farrakhan and exalt him to a level of leadership he could never have earned. "The starting point for change in black communities is not Washington, D.C., by means of a man who promotes hatred in black people," Jesse said, "the starting point for change is inside of individuals, with individuals learning self-responsibility, personal initiative and self-discipline." Everywhere Jesse traveled, voicing this criticism of the march, black audiences told him he had been duped by white people, he had been brainwashed, and he was full of self-loathing. He always responds that this line of criticism is a script that black Americans have been given by their self-serving "leaders," who use black people by nurturing their anger at whites, and who grotesquely exaggerate about racism because by so doing they magnify their own importance as the alleged saviors of black Americans.

Time and again I have seen people respond to Jesse's message of self-responsibility and individualism with intense anger and rage, always based on a misguided notion of racial fidelity. His emphasis on responsible manhood and eschewing resentment and anger is so antithetical to the prevailing message from black politicians and civil rights professionals that many people—black and white—do not know how to respond to it thoughtfully, and so they lash out with *ad hominem* attacks, which is always the easiest thing to do. From my perspective, real progress for poor black Americans will await a time when honest, thoughtful criticisms are met with honest, thoughtful reactions.

15

ARE AMERICA'S JURIES RACE-OBSESSED?

Deroy Murdock

Race Seems to Play an Increasing Role in Many Jury Verdicts
Page one headline in the *Wall Street Journal*, October 4, 1995

Does race really influence jury verdicts? All-white juries in the South used to acquit white defendants on charges of raping and lynching blacks, no matter how strong the evidence against them. Many now wonder if the glove is on the other hand. The O. J. Simpson murder case is just the latest, and most prominent, example of a growing legal trend scholars call "jury nullification" in which jurors ignore the law and judge cases based on their own personal views of justice.

JUDGMENT BY RACE?

The conventional wisdom holds that the racism of the jurors in the O. J. Simpson case propelled them to acquit the one-time football hero. The mainstream media scarcely acknowledged that, while Simpson surely seemed guilty, he correctly was presumed innocent until proven otherwise beyond a reasonable doubt. Could those tight gloves, the absence of a murder weapon, and evidence stained by its association with the truly bigoted cop, Mark

Fuhrman, have persuaded jurors that the prosecution had not surpassed the legal standard beyond which O. J. could be denied his liberty? The "racist jury" thesis also supposes that nine black jurors (with the collusion of two whites and a Hispanic) acted in racial solidarity with a black man who married a white woman, played golf, and lived on an estate in Brentwood—a long drive from the 'hood, even with the sheriff on your trail.

Simpson prosecutor Christopher Darden, of all people, doubts the jury in *The People v. O. J. Simpson* was driven by skin color. "I am not about to call this a race-based verdict," Darden told students at the University of Miami Law School. "There was a lot more to that verdict than you know."[1]

Still, in other cases that did not sink to the level of judicial Mardi Gras, it's hard not to imagine what, beyond race, might have been on the jurors' minds.

Consider the case of Lemrick Nelson. In 1991, during three days of anti-Semitic riots in Brooklyn's Crown Heights district, then sixteen-year-old Nelson was arrested for stabbing to death an Australian rabbinical student named Yankel Rosenbaum. Nelson was caught hiding in a bush with a bloody knife in his pocket and Rosenbaum's blood spattered on his clothing. Before he died, Rosenbaum identified Nelson as his assailant to police.

Despite this mound of evidence and Nelson's confession to the New York Police Department, a jury of nine blacks and three Hispanics accepted a defense theory that he had been framed by police. So they acquitted Nelson. And after rendering the verdict, the jury attended a party for Nelson and his attorneys.

In 1990, Darryl Smith was acquitted of murder in Washington, D.C. A juror contacted the court anonymously to say that, at first, a majority of jurors considered Smith guilty. But, he wrote in a letter, they eventually agreed with the other jurors who "didn't want to send any more Young Black Men to Jail."

Statistics also suggest that racial solidarity between defendants and jurors is a serious matter. In the Bronx, which is 80 percent black and Hispanic, 47.6 percent of black defendants are acquitted in felony cases—almost three times the national average of 17 percent for all races. In Wayne County, Michigan, home of mainly black Detroit, 30 percent of felony trials ended in acquittals in 1993, nearly twice the average.[2]

With O. J. Simpson now battling arthritis on the back nine, numbers such as these have raised questions about whether the jury system ought to be reformed. Some ideas to do so are fairly modest and are designed to curb the peacetime equivalent of draft-dodging: ducking jury duty. Paying significantly more than the $15 per day that jurors earn in New York City, for example, might broaden the pool of available jurors, presumably beyond those who might respond to racial appeals.

Another suggestion is for states and cities to adopt "one-day, one-trial" procedures such as those in Norfolk County, Massachusetts. If a potential juror is not assigned to a case in one day, he is free to go. This would answer the complaints of many potential jurors who can spend weeks just waiting to be selected for a trial.

Other suggestions, however, are far more ambitious. Nonunanimous convictions, for example, would send defendants to prison with only, say, ten of twelve jurors persuaded of their guilt.

POLICE CORRUPTION

But if the goal is to increase the conviction rate for criminal suspects, prosecutors and judges might focus instead on how to reverse the belief among some jurors that the police simply cannot be trusted. The fact is that some black citizens automatically discount the words of police officers who mount the witness stand. Such jurors think, erroneously, that all cops are corrupt.

The vast majority of police officers are honest, dedicated public servants who keep decent people and bloodthirsty thugs apart. But a small band of brigands can besmirch this truth. New York's "Dirty Thirty" has heaped a bucket of black ink all over a police force that has helped push violent crime down 36 percent in two years.

New York's thirtieth precinct, located in Harlem, was the site of the Big Apple's worst case of police corruption. Since 1994, thirty-five of its officers have been charged with a variety of stunning crimes. So far, sixteen have been convicted of multiple state and federal violations.

The "Dirty Thirty" were found guilty of robbing drug dealers of their narcotics, then selling those same drugs on the street. Some officers engaged in so-called key jobs where they frisked suspects, stole their house keys, and then illegally entered their apartments, robbing them of drugs, guns, and cash. A number of officers took bribes from drug dealers to look the other way or interfere when other cops tried to investigate.

One officer, George Nova, testified that he and his partner, John Arena, accepted a motorcycle, a Cadillac, and a $3,000 paint job for officer Arena's rusting Ford Bronco. In appreciation, the cops bought the drug dealer a present: a bullet-proof vest. "We wanted to give him a Christmas gift, and we didn't know what to give him," Nova explained in court. Several officers admitted that they lied to juries and judges to cover up their illegal behavior.

In Philadelphia, meanwhile, a grand jury is reviewing 100,000 cases tainted by a cadre of crooked cops. Fifty-five convictions have been overturned, including that of a fifty-seven-year-old grandmother who spent three years in prison for drug dealing. Police officers perjured themselves in her case to pressure one of her sons who was under suspicion for drug trafficking.

Tragic and maddening episodes such as these make it tougher than ever for police officers and prosecutors to maintain the respect of the public they are sworn to protect and to serve. While ethnocentrism may be flowing into America's jury boxes, keeping the cops clean is key to stemming the tide.

NOTES

1. See Christopher Darden's book, *In Contempt* (New York: HarperCollins, 1996), for Darden's full evaluation of the Simpson case.

2. For presentation and discussion of these statistics, see "Race Seems to Play an Increasing Role in Many Jury Verdicts," *Wall Street Journal,* 4 October 1995, A1.

IV

PERSPECTIVES
ON MORALS

Among the foremost concerns of black conservatives is what they understand to be the precipitous moral decline of behavioral standards in the black community. From out-of-wedlock births to black-on-black violence, the absence of strong moral expectations is a primary impediment to black mobility, much more so than structural or institutional hindrances. This section presents seven perspectives on both the practical and theoretical aspects of black conservative ethics.

In Chapter 16 Joseph H. Brown expresses the commonly held view that a moral vacuum holds much of black America in thrall, and until it is filled with sound values community progress will be slow, if it occurs at all. In Chapter 17 Diann Ellen Cameron raises the controversial question of parental licensure, suggesting that the seriousness of parental responsibility warrants the institution of a more overt public oversight of many children's home life. In Chapter 18 Steven Craft presents his inspiring personal story of religious conversion and return to moral responsibility, suggesting that such a path bears the potential for fostering a moral renascence in the lives of many Americans, black and white. Illustrating the range of black conservative ethical and social concern, Joseph E. Broadus in Chapter 19 expresses concern over the homosexual rights movement's attempt to lay claim to the moral mantle of the civil rights movement. Chapter 20 similarly focuses on a seminal issue of moral controversy, abortion. Here Peter Kir-sanow boldly denounces the abortion culture, asserting that it is morally tantamount to the institution of slavery and has an intolerably corrosive effect on the American commonweal. Chapter 21 voices Jesse Peterson's concerns over the waning moral authority of the black church; he calls ministers to abandon the surrender of their pulpits to politically correct politics and instead return to their evangelical vocation. In Chapter 22 Stan Faryna uniquely reflects on the ethical character of black conservatism, using the thought of Thomas Aquinas as a philosophical foundation.

In a postmodern age when talk of objective values and truth is seen as either intolerant or quaint, the forthrightness and moral backbone of black conservatives is refreshing. This section bears witness to the principled moral concern of those unwilling to bow to the spirit of their age.

16

The Moral Vacuum in Black America Must Be Filled

Joseph H. Brown

If one cannot govern oneself, how can all of us collectively govern either ourselves or the republic? Character is necessary to release the spiritual energy for self-government.

Michael Novak, theologian

He returned as a hero, not as the convicted rapist he is. Mike Tyson, former heavyweight boxing champion, was the recipient of all kinds of hosannas at a Harlem rally in his honor following his release from prison. Predictably, the crowd absolved him of his crime and made yet another victim of "the system" instead.

What was most damaging about this spectacle was the letter of support Tyson received from fifty-two churches. So in addition to the many prominent "leaders" who unsurprisingly wished him well such as Al Sharpton, Percy Sutton (former Manhattan borough president), and Benjamin Hooks (former head of the NAACP), many black ministers in the community also heaped praise on the convicted former champ.

MORAL DECLINE

Black ministers used to be the moral and spiritual leaders of black communities. It was they who would shake their fingers at those who weren't on the straight and narrow path of righteousness. It was they who would admonish those who crossed the line between right and wrong. But this is increasingly not the case.

It would have been appropriate if some ministers had joined a group of black people who held a vigil against violence toward women, but their moral cowardice wouldn't allow them. The entire affair was symbolic of the moral decay that has engulfed the black community during the last three decades. Thirty years ago a black man, heavyweight champion or not, could never have raped a woman, be totally unrepentant for his act, and then have a rally in his honor upon his release, as did Mike Tyson. Look at Jack Johnson, the first black heavyweight champ. His public behavior, which included drunkenness and cavorting with white women, was deemed unacceptable by leaders like Booker T. Washington. That is why when Joe Louis became the second black man to hold that title in 1937, he promised to conduct himself in such a manner that the race could be proud of him in and out of the ring. But no such code of conduct exists anymore. As the words of the Cole Porter song convey, "anything goes." Nature, proverbially speaking, abhors a vacuum, and what we have today in many black communities is a moral vacuum.

This moral vacuum was created more by silence than by anything else. There is not enough righteous anger and public denouncement of things like black-on-black homicide, open-air drug dealing, and irresponsible parenting. We do not condemn these evils the way we should. Even when racism and segregation were in their heyday, it was never like this. So when did it start? I believe we have to go back thirty years to the Moynihan Report to get the answer.

SILENCE ABOUT SOCIAL PATHOLOGIES

Thirty years ago, Daniel Patrick Moynihan spoke the perfect truth when he said: "From the wild Irish slums of the 19th century Eastern seaboard to the riot-torn suburbs of Los Angeles, there is one unmistakable lesson in American history. A community that allows a large number of young men to grow up in broken families, dominated by women, never acquiring any rational expectations about the future—that community asks for and gets chaos."[1]

Moynihan's remarks were a call to arms. As assistant secretary of labor in 1965, he saw all of the signs and issued a report warning of the consequences if the trend continued. At that time, the social climate was generally temperate—by today's standards. Out-of-wedlock births and drugs were far less pervasive. But cracks were beginning to appear in the black community's ethical and moral fortifications.

Rather than take Moynihan seriously and begin to patch up those cracks, black ministers, intellectuals, and community leaders circled the wagons in defense. They denounced both the message and the messenger. They revised history and said that single-parent black families were a residual effect of slavery. It was the beginning of the code of silence of declining moral standards in black America. The cracks in our ethical foundations soon became gaping holes.

The voices of righteousness have been muted for over thirty years now. Black ministers, civil rights leaders, and scholars have formed what political scientist Martin Kilson called an ethic *cordon sanitaire* around the black experience in America. They have basically adopted what amounts to a code of silence on such touchy issues as black crime, unwed parenthood, and inferior academic performance. These disappointments are either blamed on white racism or simply ignored. Blacks who break this code and question this official story are labeled "traitors," and whites who address these problems are automatically presumed "racist."

The result is a psychological slavery to replace the chattel form under which black Americans once suffered. The victimhood that goes along with this new form of enslavement is in many ways more devastating than its predecessor. In the slavery of old, most blacks looked for ways to escape. With the new form, many believe that they are permanently trapped in their current socioeconomic situation.

It is most disappointing to see and hear the so-called black leaders when they address the many social ills that afflict the black community. Their lack of vision, their unwillingness to publicly stand firm against self-destructive behavior, their moral cowardice, their refusal to foster self-reliance, and their blatant worship of popularity is simply appalling.

For example, everyone knows that low-income babies born out of wedlock stand a better than average chance of always living in poverty, and that these mothers virtually condemn themselves and their children to a lifetime of hardship. You don't need Moynihan's report to know this, just common sense. Yet, the so-called leaders lack the nerve and sense of morality to tackle this issue. Why? Because such talk is unpopular and would take away from the notion that all of this is the fault of the white man. "We can't let white folks off the hook," they say. But we black Americans are the ones left hanging.

If these same "leaders" who are always on the scene when a racial incident takes place would instead go on the stump about illegitimacy and other issues that lead to self-destruction, many black girls would pay attention. And some would change their behavior. But these same racial-political ambulance chasers won't do that because they don't want to be accused of putting down "the people."

Think about what a difference it would make if ministers and other traditional community leaders stopped complaining and started telling young black men to take care of their children, to take school seriously, that crime is wrong under any circumstances, and to take any job, even minimum wage, rather than be unemployed for any long period of time. It would change the moral climate in a way that no government social program ever could. But none of these officials wants to be accused of saying anything negative about black people, and so they leave it out of their public agenda.

Instead they do what Reverend Jesse Jackson did in August 1995. He led a march to the Cook County Jail in my hometown of Chicago, a structure that incarcerates over 9,000 inmates, most of whom are black. There he and others demanded a national urban policy that emphasizes jobs and education over the "jail-industry complex." Jackson's march is an example of the continued use of protest politics rather than emphasis on individual responsibility. By demanding that the government provide jobs and self-esteem to young black men instead of these same leaders going out into the community themselves and rallying the masses with appeals to pride and heritage, they prove that they are either unable or unwilling to lead.

Black America is currently deprived of the ability to solve many of its problems because there is a reluctance even to talk about them. Hewing to the old adage of not airing one's "dirty laundry" in public has harmed us to the point that we remain silent even though an orgy of self-destruction is going on right under our noses. But how can dirty laundry become clean unless it's taken out of the hamper? Sadly, avoiding bad press has taken precedence over solving problems, and we suffer for it.

The moral vacuum that currently exists in black America must be filled. We simply cannot continue to live like this. It is beneath our heritage. We must know that there is no hope for us to change without concerted moralizing. We must distinguish behavior that is self-evidently wrong from that which is self-evidently right. If as a people we insist on being too bashful to say out loud what we know to be true—that the advancement of the race hinges on a reaffirmation of personal responsibility and moral law—then we will continue to pay the price. And all of those black Americans who died—during centuries of fierce struggle—in order to make us free and to enable us to take our rightful place in this society, will have perished in vain. We cannot let that happen.

NOTE

1. See Daniel Patrick Moynihan, *The Black Family: The Case for National Action* (Washington, D.C.: Superintendent of Documents, 1965).

17

THE BLACK FAMILY AND PARENTAL LICENSURE

Diann Ellen Cameron

[Family is] the center of social life, and . . . the locus of formation of personal character.

Glenn Loury, economist

It was another typical day at my job. I work at a private, black foster care and adoption agency that specializes in meeting the needs of black and Latino children. Kevin,[1] a ten-year-old boy, was finally going home with a black family who wanted to adopt him. After several meetings between Kevin and the family, I watched him leave the agency to venture to his new home—and, hopefully his final placement. He seemed happy and as settled as one could be after being shuffled in and out of foster homes for over the past three years.

As he walked out of the door, one of our new foster parents brought in a two-week-old baby girl for her initial medical exam. (She was eventually named Carla by her foster parents.) Carla was released from a local hospital and directly placed in foster care by city child welfare officials. She was born addicted to cocaine and opiates, and infected with syphilis. The foster parent was a gentle black woman. She and her husband—both professionals—welcomed this child into their home. The Mitchells would shower young Carla with a bounty of love and attention, until her mother could eventually (if ever possible) care for her. Yet, the Mitchells probably would never fully comprehend Carla's gratitude or the appreciation of the social worker for the tremendous effort they would undertake. Carla was the eighth "positive-tox" baby we placed in a foster boarding home that week. Overall, our total tally of foster children had reached a disheartening 1,200—95 percent of whom were black.

THE BLACK FAMILY

The black family is the most important institution in our community, second only to the black church and other spiritual sanctuaries preserved by our diverse black American culture. This institution—the family—is responsible for educating our children and providing for their physical, emotional, and social needs. It is the primary source of personal development and character formation. Its foundation of nurturance, discipline, and promotion of learning strengthens a child's future ability to contribute to the general welfare of the community and society at large. The black family, as any other family, is a sovereign entity established by God to maintain social order and preserve our culture and humanity. But tragically, the black family today is beset with serious challenges that threaten its structure and viability in the new millennium.

Some challenges to the black family are from significant external forces. Racism/discrimination, impoverished living conditions, and homelessness, as well as rising community violence, play meaningful roles in the black family's ability to seize the socioeconomic opportunities necessary to its survival and success. However, the continued threats from *within* the black family will have serious consequences for its children and our community, and are in fact the most daunting forces confronting it. These threats include, but are not limited to, adult drug and alcohol addiction, domestic violence, out-of-wedlock births, and nonwork. The family environments that result contribute significantly to a disproportionate number of black children who are being *institutionally* harvested into foster care, group homes, juvenile prisons, and neonatal wards (to wean off crack-cocaine).

Between 1982 and 1990, the number of black children requiring separation from their biological families leaped from 34 percent in 1982 to 40 percent in 1990.[2] Black children led the "substitute care" population of approximately 500,000 nationwide. Nearly two-thirds were living in foster care placements, and another 15 percent were in group homes, emergency shelters, or other noncorrectional facilities. The remaining small population of foster children from our communities reside in either hospitals or some form of correctional institutions.[3]

Black children increasingly bear the burden of a community seemingly unable to address the issue of parental and family responsibility. A disproportionate amount of energy is spent on changing and thwarting external variables. Instead, such efforts should be equally placed on confronting the harmful choices made by many black adults that consistently put our children in peril—brutally abusing one's child, sexually violating a child, or exposing our children to the damaging effects of drug use while in utero.

Currently, there is a continued movement to broaden the liability against parents and hold them accountable for injurious actions committed against children. Criminal and family court cases across the nation demonstrate a clear national trend to protecting children from their parents.[4] This includes abuse, abandonment, and poor supervision, all conditions that raise the likelihood of a child's delinquency. The question remains—can the black community solve its own problems, or must we allow federal and state policies to reshape, redefine, and reconstruct our families, and hence, ourselves?

PARENTAL LICENSURE?

The movement toward parental licensure is more than thirty years old. Social philosophers saw the decline in quality of life as one result of disorganized families, drug abuse, and crime, and so began suggesting the licensure of parents. It was not long before psychologists and even politicians conceded that the way children are parented strongly influences our nation's quality of life and social status.

The growth in foster care placements, juvenile delinquency, crime, and increase in homicide among youth (especially black) set the stage for continued efforts to hold parents accountable for the devastation suffered by children. No longer would the rearing of children by their biological parents be considered a *private* matter.

The cornerstone of this movement is twofold: (1) the family's right to privacy is not a constitutional guarantee; and (2) parenthood and the freedom to rear a child is a privilege rather than a biological right. In other words, this privilege is defined by life experiences, investment in the child, and quality parent-child relationships—not automatically designated by the event of childbirth alone.

There are three significant reasons why some black Americans and others support the movement to "license parents" or increase parental liability.

These reasons are simply (1) costs to the child; (2) costs to our community; and (3) costs to our posterity.

In the black community, the costs to the children caused by negligent or abusive parenting are staggering. Physical abuse not only damages a child physically and psychologically, but it also teaches a child that violence—unbridled and unyielding—is the solution to a conflict or meeting a need. Of course, sexual abuse can impair children both psychologically and socially, often causing them to constantly relive the traumatic abuse through either self-destructive ways or by victimizing others. Manifestations of these behaviors might include habitual drug use, sexual promiscuity, or molestation of younger children. Finally, abandonment is a serious event in a child's life that can inhibit a child from building cohesive relationships and developing a strong sense of identity and self-esteem. Forms of physical abuse, sexual abuse, or parental abandonment can cost our children their ability to live well-adjusted, social stable lives. And of course, the greater prevalence of these events among a people, the greater the damage done to them as a whole.

We know that improper family functioning is strongly linked to delinquent juvenile behavior, which inadvertently affects the quality of life in the whole. Crime, dependence on public welfare, a proliferation of emerging families headed by teen parents, and a continued decline in educational achievements have all become serious burdens for black communities to repair and salvage. Failure at this task causes our community to come still further under siege by violent acts and lawlessness. A vicious cycle develops, decreasing the quality of the law-abiding black residents.

Those who support proposals for parental licensing maintain that these social conditions warrant licensure to protect children. This concept is neither new nor unreasonable, as almost every other aspect of family life is regulated. Parents of children who fail to be adequate parents—and this failure becomes publicly known—often lose their children. This is why the foster care system is so busy. Similarly, the right to be a foster parent, adoptive parent, youth mentor, or child care provider is incumbent on "passing the test." Enormous emphasis is placed on choosing the "right" persons to raise someone else's child, when, sadly, no concern is given as to how children are raised by those who conceived them. The parental licensure movement is a reasonable reaction to the growing decline in the quality of families and the increased evidence of incompetent parenting. Too many families in the black community fit this profile. Therefore, the greater black community must intervene and restore itself to prevent any further decline in the quality of black family life.

STRENGTHENING THE BLACK FAMILY

Not one family within the black community is a private entity; each family unit contributes to our community's well-being for better or for worse. Therefore, every aspect within the black community is needed to protect and preserve the black family as an institution. Churches, civic groups, community merchants, and residents themselves bear a responsibility for maintaining healthy families within the community. Furthermore, members of the black community must ensure that each family unit has the proper elements—parental stability, parent-child cohesiveness, and an environment filled with the proper balance of nurturance and discipline, to increase a family's social opportunity.

Visible, consistent involvement in each other's family affairs reinforces our community and prevents any further family dissolution within black America. No longer can the members of our community sit idly by and allow our fate and future to be determined or prejudged by others. We must be diligent in becoming foster parents, adoptive parents, and benefactors to adolescent youth living in group homes or other residential communities. These are several ways we can strengthen our children and create more stable families for our future. Also, we must not ignore the black extended-family network (grandparents, aunts/uncles, godparents, and friends), since it is the primary preserver of family history and resources within our community.

Furthermore, our neighborhood organizations should expand on their family and youth programs, giving many parents assistance in caring for and supervising their children. One way of achieving this is the incorporation of "community trusts" within each black district. This would create ancillary funding for residents' needs and provide the means to rebuild the community's infrastructure, while stimulating its economy.

Through creative self-reliance we can institute a parenting/family agenda within the black community, without the intrusion of regulatory bodies. However, it must first begin with the firm commitment that abuse, neglect, and family violence have no place within the black community and are utterly dissonant with our heritage.

Only the members of our community can determine the fate of our culture. This fate rests in the strength, solidarity, and wealth of moral fiber within black families. Whether it is an urban or a rural community, black families are the barometer of our collective success or failure. In order to strengthen and protect our children, we must understand that the black family is an institution that we should continually strengthen and preserve through our collective resources. Vulnerable families among us must be able to find supportive resources and services from within the black community. Without this connection on a human service/community development level, the black family runs the risk of being further defined and shaped by governmental policies and statutes . . . and even the possibility of parental licensing.

NOTES

1. This is a pseudonym, as are all other first and last names used in this essay referring to people involved in the foster system.

2. H. N. Snyder and M. Sickmund, *Juvenile Offenders and Victims: A National Report* (Washington, D.C.: Office of Juvenile Justice and Delinquency Prevention, U.S. Department of Justice, 1995).

3. Ibid.

4. See J. C. Westman, *Licensing Parents: Can We Prevent Child Abuse and Neglect?* (New York: Insight Books, 1994).

18

A Setback Is a Setup for a Comeback

Steven Craft

Amazing grace, how sweet the sound, that saved a wretch like me;
I once was lost, but now am found; was blind, but now I see.

John Newton

My own comeback from a former life of crime is proof that it is possible to change the behavior of a criminal. The changes that have occurred in my own life demonstrate—in my opinion, beyond a shadow of a doubt—that a criminal can change his heart by becoming a morally mature, intelligent, and successful person who can both effectively love and work.

But these sorts of changes cannot simply be accounted for by political or socioeconomic factors, because a person is a spiritual and moral being, not simply a machine that can be manipulated by external forces. Socially and psychologically oriented crime experts rarely talk about this beautiful dimension of the person, but it exists, and powerfully so.

An Internal Problem

Criminal behavior is in many dimensions a spiritual and moral problem, and it proceeds from the condition of the criminal's person. It is a condition characterized by the lack of understanding of who one is, of proper values in relation to truth, and of self-responsibility. By not realizing that we are more than our everyday social and political interaction, we fail to see that we have opportunities to pursue moral and spiritual improvement. Because we do not acknowledge that we are called upon to live each day gently and virtuously, we as a result become confused, and it is in this confusion that our worst tendencies come out.

Those who feel that humans are decidedly good fail to explain the things that humans do that are decidedly wrong. These people, while accepting the idea that people have both the opportunities and resources to do good, fail to understand that we have the opportunities and internal inclinations to do terrible things as well. A theological truth that echoes this fact is the scripture that states: "For from within, out of the heart of men, proceed evil thoughts, adulteries, fornications, murders, thefts, covetousness, wickedness, etc., all these evil things come from within and defile the man" (Mark 7: 21–23). Not just the Bible, but any current newspaper provides proof that people are capable of terrible and violent actions.

Therefore, if we want to mitigate crime, we must change the way we think about criminals and the way criminals think about ourselves. First and foremost, it is vital to understand that people are not good without sincere effort. We cannot be gentle and virtuous without truly striving for goodness, and even then sound guidance is essential. Just "doing time" will not change the criminal, and neither will any form of punishment for its own sake. But a change in the heart and mind of the criminal can be accomplished through spiritual and moral regeneration. As a former heroin addict, I've committed crimes in order to support my drug habit, and when I did so I did not feel the threat of punishment was strong enough to deter me from committing crime. Nor, in my experience, do social programs effectively rehabilitate criminals, at least not without a change in the criminal's own heart.

Certainly, it is necessary to incarcerate criminals in order to keep them off the streets, preying on innocent and law-abiding citizens. However, rather than just recycling criminals back into society at the end of their sentence, we must work toward the moral and spiritual regeneration in their lives in order to effect permanent change. If we want to see the reform of criminals, we must bring the word of God into the prisons. Ultimately, it is the light that shines forth from the Cross which can break the hardened hearts of criminals and let them see the wonder that a Christian life brings. This approach has historically been integral to black community life, and we as a people need to reassert this ennobling tradition.

THE VALUE OF BIBLICAL INFLUENCE

I was born to Louis and Adele Craft on October 10, 1943, in New Brunswick, New Jersey. I am the oldest of three children raised in a conservative, working-class family. Living through the era of Jim Crow segregation, I remember that we were all taught a strong Judeo-Christian value system. This was an important source of moral strength for us. Although the Jim Crow days were hard times for black Americans, it brought black folks together and gave us all the same concerns. Having to live in oppression and racism caused cohesion among black Americans—rich and poor, we lived together and held the Bible tightly together. For it was through the Bible that we knew ourselves to be equal as human beings, to be loved and cherished by God, and to be individually striving for a good and moral life. The Bible, not our circumstances, was our moral authority.

Even though the Bible's powerful and vital insights were deeply ingrained, I came to embrace crime and immorality in my twenties. I turned away from the Bible's insights at a time when the black American condition had decidedly improved: the 1960s. The 1960s came with a thrill of the times and the excitement of civil liberties. This excitement spilled over into how we lived our lives and how we thought about things. This excitement also became a confusion out of which developed a selfishness that grasped for meaning. Later, this confusion turned into desperation and emptiness. Like so many black Americans, just as doors were opening that had long been closed, I was limiting myself by leaving the biblically grounded moral heritage of my people.

I should not have failed in this way. I graduated from New Brunswick High School in June 1961, and was nurtured on the Lord's Prayer, daily Bible readings, the Ten Commandments, as well as the Pledge of Allegiance. The values associated with these acts served my generation well by giving us an awareness of the Creator and the knowledge of right from wrong. Upon graduation from high school, I found a clerical position at a stock brokerage firm named Bache & Company on New York City's Wall Street. The values of thrift and prudence I had learned as a high school student served me well, and I wisely budgeted my $100 a week. Biblical morality had prepared me to succeed in society.

THE EFFECT OF THE SIXTIES

But though I had these good habits, I was unprepared for the social storms that were on their way. By the mid-1960s, the massive social revolution began in American society. A Supreme Court decision removed school prayer and Bible readings from the public schools, and values-clarification and moral relativism took their place. The civil rights, Black Power, women's, and hippie movements were out to change American social structures, and they had substantial influence. Some changes—such as the end of legal racial discrimination—were, of course, long overdue; others, however, were unrealistic and ideological in nature. In any event, the words used by these groups were frustrating and confusing, and I and many other young black men experienced anger.

The ideas proposed during the 1960s incensed and stirred all young people across America. It took time and reflection for me to understand that these ideas were not always the best way to proceed with change. But I was young, and I felt it was a time to act. So rage and rebellion gripped my heart as the nation struggled with issues of race, poverty, injustice, drugs, and war. There was an optimistic belief in the unlimited possibilities that change could produce, and at that time it was very exciting to be part of these changes.

Consequently, I began to systematically reject the Judeo-Christian values that I had grown up with as a child. They had been portrayed to me as bigoted and stifling, a part of the problem, not a part of the solution. I began to embrace a philosophy of life that was based on hatred, bitterness, and rage against the "system." I rejected my Christian upbringing because, I was told, it produced inequalities and racism. I was convinced by the teachings of Malcolm X and the Black Panthers that the white race was the enemy of black people everywhere. Furthermore, I was persuaded that Christianity was nothing more than the "white man's religion," a tool used to oppress and enslave black people.

In June 1964, I resigned from my job on Wall Street in order to join the United States Army. I did this because I was classified "A-1" in the draft and would have been put on orders for combat service in Vietnam—yet another example of the same racism that made me so angry. But instead of combat duty, I was sent to Fort Campbell, Kentucky. There I served as a company clerk in the 557 Combat Engineer Corps. Imbued with the spirit of my age, I despised the discipline of the military and began to rebel against authority by using drugs and alcohol on a regular basis. I saw myself as an "oppressed victim" of American society, and by the time I was discharged, in 1966, I was a full-fledged alcoholic and drug addict. Rage and bitterness had induced self-destructive habits in me.

A LIFE OF CRIME

From 1964 to 1977, I was caught in a vise-grip of crimes ranging from theft, burglary, and forgery to drug-dealing. These crimes were committed in order to support my heroin habit of approximately $100 per day. My partner in crime was my cousin, Jimmy. He was also my teacher. Jimmy taught me how to burglarize apartment buildings, push drugs, shoplift in major department stores, and "hustle" in New York City. He was a very influential, though negative, role model for me: I looked up to him as a "city-slicker" from the Big Apple. Jimmy was a heroin addict, and he eventually died from an overdose of heroin in a New York "shooting gallery," a place where addicts congregated to inject drugs. His abandonment of Judeo-Christian morality did not serve him well either.

Looking back on this nightmarish time in my life, I recall my mixed emotions of fear of arrest, of exhilaration at getting away with a crime and "scoring" drugs, and of excitement at "getting high" on heroin and cocaine. I cannot remember many vivid details about that drug-induced madness, but I do know that the cycle of drug addiction, crime, incarceration, and secular social work programs such as Phoenix House and Methadone Maintenance did not change my basic emptiness and desperation. With my emptiness unfilled, there could be no change in the way I lived and how I thought.

During this "setback era," I found my life going through profound changes. I was recycled in and out of the criminal justice system. Each time I was released from a jail term, I would try in my own strength to avoid drugs, but found myself powerless to overcome the craving and compulsion associated with drug addiction and alcoholism. It was this experience that had convinced me that permanent change cannot happen in the lives of drug-enslaved criminals without a spiritual and moral regeneration of heart. The emptiness and desperation demand to be filled, and without the proper diet of faith, real and lasting rehabilitation is impossible.

For example, in 1972, I relocated to Los Angeles, California, from New York City, believing that the change of environment would help straighten me out. This proved to be a false belief, and I began to realize that the problems of my drug abuse and criminal behavior were internal rather than external. I simply transported the problems with me to another location! When the stress and pressures of daily living would weigh me down, I would revert back to my "comfort zone." I escaped reality and my real problems by getting high. At least, I kept these unpleasantries out of my mind for periods of time through the use of drugs. This, in turn, would begin the cycle of drug addiction and criminality all over again. These repeated experiences—shared universally by so many addicts—further convinced me that simply recycling criminals through the criminal justice system is futile.

CONVERSION

In 1977, I went into a drug-induced psychosis on Venice Beach, California. I had been drinking 100-proof rum, smoking P.C.P., and shooting cocaine, and then I passed out. I do not know what happened, but when I awoke, I found myself in the back of an ambulance, restrained in a straight-jacket and on my way to the Camarillo State Hospital.

I was committed to the hospital for temporary insanity, and it was a frightening time. Lying there helpless, I was shocked to open my eyes and find the shining light of the Cross filling my view. Through this profound experience, I saw the need for spiritual help from God. I admitted to my Creator that I had no power to overcome drug and alcohol addiction in my life. I recognized and admitted that only a power greater than myself could restore me to sanity.

I turned my life and will over to God and let Him into my life. I followed His guidance, and He gave me courage and grace enough to meet my personal challenges—the spiritual and moral defects of my own character. Through Christ's love, I began to accept full responsibility for my criminal behavior and to take personal inventory of my shortcomings. That week I spent in the hospital changed my heart and mind, and I could again feel that God was near to me.

After the hospital released me, I joined a black charismatic church and began to grow spiritually and morally. I did not return to my old ways of responding to stress and pressure, but instead applied daily self-discipline, restraint, personal responsibility, and Christian principles for a full six-month period without reverting to drugs and alcohol.

By the middle of 1978, I had found employment in Los Angeles driving a taxicab and doing part-time custodial work. It was hard work, but it was honest. I continued to attend church services regularly, and I began to date Edith Austin, whom I married a few months later. We have been married sixteen years now and have two children, aged fifteen and ten.

I was now moving toward the next period in my life, which I will call the "setup era"; this started in 1978 and lasted until 1990. During this time, my life began to take on new meaning as I consistently applied the spiritual principles that I was learning in church: The importance of a strong family unit was impressed in my heart, and I worked hard to improve my standard of living.

Our lives became enriched as we met new friends through the church, and I began to develop new patterns of thinking about, and relating to, life's problems. No longer was I bitter and angry at the "white man's system." Daily I found inner peace and strength to overcome the temptation to return to drugs and alcohol, because I had truly changed on the inside rather than merely being patched up on the outside. I was a new person, with a reliable moral compass.

During the "setup period" of my life, I came to the conclusion that the same experience that was working for me could work for others as well. I truly was "free at last." No longer did I need dope to function. No longer did I have to commit crimes to support that awful habit. No longer did I have to worry about losing my mind to drug-induced psychosis. No longer did I have to worry about incarceration and premature death.

I was free from that bondage, and I was being "set up" by my Creator for a higher purpose in life. I was given a testimony of hope to inspire others. My mind was being renewed, and my message of hope was the declaration that anger, bitterness, self-hatred, and destructive behavior were replaceable by self-control, forgiveness, love, and respect for others. No longer was I being overcome by evil, but I was learning daily how to overcome evil with good. Looking back at that "setup era" in my life, I can clearly see how my life was being reestablished in the traditional moral values of the black community, and it was a direct result of spiritual and moral regeneration.

COMEBACK

In 1990, I felt a calling to prepare to go into the ministry. Financially speaking, my wife and I knew this would create hardship. Nevertheless, we had a firm belief that this was the right time to proceed, and I enrolled in Central Bible College in Springfield, Missouri. After completing my bachelor's degree in pastoral ministry in 1993, I began work on a master's degree at Harvard University School of Divinity in Cambridge, Massachusetts. I graduated in 1996, and my wife also graduated the same year with a bachelor's degree in elementary education.

It is truly liberating to see and tell others that they can go from the pit to the palace, if they let God change their lives. I can look back over my life today and say to the criminal drug addict that there is hope and restoration. I am a living example of the power of spiritual regeneration, having been free from drugs, alcohol, and crime for over sixteen years. Currently, I work as a student intern in the prison system in Massachusetts, telling my story and letting the inmates know that a "setback is a setup for a comeback." I tell them they can change, and rehabilitation can work if it is true spiritual regeneration, rather than only rote government social work programs that do not address the spiritual and moral nature of drug addiction and crime.

As I look back and draw on the lessons from my own experience, a few principles come to mind. First, I had to admit that I was powerless to overcome drugs and alcohol and that my life had become unmanageable. Second, I came to believe that a power greater than myself could restore me to sanity. Then I made a decision to turn my life over to Him. Next, I took a sincere moral inventory of my life and began to take full responsibility for my personal behavior, rather than blame it on history or the behavior of other people.

I asked God to begin the process of regeneration and restoration. In time, I developed a daily relationship with my Creator and consistently cooperated with Him by refusing to revert to my former lifestyle. Finally, this commitment gave me the spiritual strength to overcome my addiction and to share with others who are struggling the message that they can also be truly free.

We, as black Americans, must help our children and our neighbors' children avoid the kind of problems that I and so many like me created. These days, children are increasingly at risk for drug addiction and criminal behavior. Early intervention and prevention are critical through strong family units, relationship with a church, and safe and inspiring communities. We also need to return sound moral teaching to schools. These are things that we should be working together to accomplish. These are the things that we should be talking about in our communities and with our governors, senators, and congressmen. It is time to bring back a moral consensus into the black community. We should rediscover our self-understanding as human beings who are loved by God, who know right from wrong, and who are self-responsible. With this rediscovery we will recover the life-giving institutions of the family, the church, and the community. And it is with these institutions that we will discover both success and achievement.

19

FAMILY VALUES VS. HOMOSEXUAL RIGHTS: TRADITION COLLIDES WITH AN ELITE SOCIAL TIDE

Joseph E. Broadus

A substantial sector of the black community is suffering because so much of the energy and driving force of the movement have been deflected toward Hispanic Americans, middle-class white women [and] homosexuals. . . . Don't forget, the civil rights movement started out with blacks . . . [and they are] losing ground at each displacing development.

Kenneth Tollett, professor, Howard University

In an increasingly common political occurrence today, advocates for greater legal recognition and protection for homosexual lifestyles argue that their movement represents a natural progression of the civil rights movement. Arguing from an individual rights perspective, they link their cause to the broader crusades for civil rights for minorities and women, thereby suggesting the normalcy of their lifestyle. This strategy, though effective, is an affront to many black Americans, who with their strong religious roots and traditional view of family stand against the normativity of homosexuality.[1]

SECOND THOUGHTS

The early success to date of homosexual activists can in large part be traced to the broad acceptance of both the civil rights and the "sexual freedom" movements among the country's elites—professors, opinion-makers, artists, and so on. While certainly the civil rights movement is worthy, it is not so generally clear that the movement for "sexual freedom" has equal merit. The faltering of these movements in recent years can be linked to growing doubts about both the expanse of civil rights regulation and the negative effects of the sexual revolution. These movements, which earlier surfed a rising and popular wave of social reform, are now caught in the undercurrent of reappraisal.[2]

This is especially true of the homosexual rights campaign. While at one time the comparability of the homosexual rights movement with the black civil rights movement seemed obvious to many, now a growing chorus of critics see the homosexual rights drive merely as a weak, politically correct imitation. The spectre of AIDS and other sexually transmitted diseases, as well as the family breakup often associated with the sexual revolution, has stifled this forced relationship between blacks and homosexuals.

This sea change has been brought about by a number of other forces. Certainly, the often underrecognized traditional family bent of black Americans is a significant one. But so is the rise of a transracial populist American conservatism. This collection of social conservatives, religious conservatives, immigrants, and political moderates questions the appropriateness of elite-dominated institutions (e.g., film, journalism, the academy) supplanting traditional values—such as heterosexual monogamy and the marriage-based two-parent family—with their own private preferences. The resulting social, sexual, and moral counterrevolution is at the core of the American culture wars.

THE CLAIM

The proponents of specialized civil rights protection based on sexual orientation frequently argue that their movement is the latest phase in social and constitutional evolution. They claim that a process has been set in order that has seen American society expand the concept of full citizenship from the special rights of white males to an increasing list, which includes African Americans, women, Native Americans, and now gay, lesbian, and bisexual individuals. They maintain that the social norm of equality and the specialized norms of our civil rights laws should protect them.

This is, most basically, a moral claim, as it assumes no moral difficulty with homosexual activity and life. Obviously this idea is not uncontroversial. At a minimum, the operating assumption of proponents of homosexual special rights—and they are "special" rights, as all homosexuals, and citizens in general, are already covered by existing civil rights laws—is that homosexual activities fail to make significant statements about character and moral worth. This would rank it as a morally neutral trait; hence, it should not be proscribed or disapproved of in any way.

THE REALITY

Importantly, the unacknowledged reality of the homosexual rights movement is that it is different from other civil rights movements. The goal of other movements has been to remove the disabilities imposed by governmental limitations on the rights of oppressed social groups to participate in the opportunities of society. But homosexuals are not an oppressed group— quite the contrary, in fact. They are largely an elite class, with higher levels of education and income than most segments of the population. They are, on the whole, significantly more privileged than conventional, heterosexual Americans.[3]

The real subtext of much of the work of the sexual orientation reformers and homosexual activists is not simply to secure the tolerance or acceptance of a small number of homosexuals, but rather to effect a wholesale transformation of the sexual norms of society, so that the traditional becomes stigmatized and the aberrant normative. They seek to use government regulation as a tool to reshape society. The identification with the historic civil rights movement is deployed to this end, because its moral pedigree is unassailable. But black Americans are increasingly uncomfortable with this equation, feeling as though they are being used; obviously, this is a very unsettling thought for an African American. It may well be that the family-centered traditions of black Americans will pose a most formidable roadblock to this elite movement's future.

NOTES

1. For an insightful analysis of this political strategy of homosexual rights groups, see Elizabeth Wright, "In the Name of 'Civil Rights,'" *Issues and Views* (spring 1996):3.

2. For discussion of the effects on the black underclass of the moral revolution of the 1960s, led by many of the same elites who support the mainstreaming of homosexuality, see generally Myron Magnet, *The Dream and the Nightmare: The Sixties' Legacy to the Underclass* (New York: William Morrow, 1993).

3. See, generally, Wright, "In the Name of 'Civil Rights'"; Jerry Z. Muller, "Coming Out Ahead: The Homosexual Moment in the Academy," *First Things*

(August/September 1993); Robert H. Bork, *Slouching Towards Gomorrah* (New York: HarperCollins, 1996), esp. 103–104, 112–114; Dinesh D'Souza, *Illiberal Education* (New York: Free Press, 1991), esp. 242–243; Magnet, *The Dream and the Nightmare*, 136, 213–214.

20

A BLACK CONSERVATIVE
LOOKS AT ABORTION

Peter Kirsanow

Before I formed you in the womb, I knew you, and before you were born I consecrated you.

Jeremiah 1:5

[How] can [we] look our daughters in the eye and tell them that it is somehow consistent with freedom for them to trample on the human rights of their unborn offspring[?]. We're going to have to find the courage one of these days to tell people that freedom is not an easy discipline. Freedom is not a choice for those who are lazy in their heart and in their respect for their own moral capacities. Freedom requires that at the end of the day you accept the constraint that is required ... a respect for the laws of nature and nature's God that say unequivocally that your daughters do not have the right to do what is wrong, that [your] sons do not have the right to do what is wrong. They do not have the right to steal bread from the mouths of the innocent, they do not have the right to steal life from the womb of the unborn.

Dr. Alan Keyes

Abortion is the seminal issue of our time. No single subject produces such virulent, bitter discord as abortion. It turns citizens into fanatics, judges into autocrats, and politicians into cowards. And, like it or not, it is the defining issue for black conservatism, in the same way that slavery was the defining issue for the nascent Republican party. Indeed, many commentators have referred to the fractious debate over abortion as America's current Civil War.[1] A few others have gone beyond mere analogy and have predicted that the conflict will erupt into actual civil strife.

But while such Civil War rhetoric may be hyperbolic, there remains an inescapable nexus between that great struggle and the struggle over abortion. The Civil War and its legislative aftermath affirmed the humanity of black slaves, entitled to equal protection under the law. The abortion debate, in the end, is about the humanity of the unborn child and whether such a child is endowed with certain inalienable rights, foremost among them the right to life.

Yet amidst our social sound and fury about abortion, even the most pedestrian analysis vividly demonstrates the humanity of the unborn child. The old method of process of elimination suffices: The child in the womb is not inanimate; it is not a dog or a cat, or other mammal; neither is it a reptile, fish, or bird; it is not any form of vegetation; neither is it a bacterium or virus; it is not an organ of the mother. Left to develop without interruption, the unborn child will be born human and nothing else. This basic point presents a quandary for pro-abortion forces. Just as slavery was justified on the basis that blacks were not human, the abortion industry largely depends on the fiction that the unborn child is somehow not quite human.

FETUS AND SLAVE: NOT FULLY HUMAN

The primary tactic in the systematic abuse of any class of people is to dehumanize them. Thus, it cannot be admitted that the unborn child is a person, and it cannot be granted that the unborn child has inalienable rights, including the right to life. A concession that the unborn child is a person would destroy the psychology of denial that makes the decision to abort easier. The identical constructs were used to support slavery. Every attempt was made to deny that blacks were fully human. They didn't look like "us," so they must not be "us." Their humanity could not be allowed to become a public reality. Masters in some colonies were even prohibited from freeing slaves, since to do so might suggest a moral problem with slavery and somehow communicate the humanity of the enslaved.

Slaves were often considered and treated as real estate in some areas and as personal property in others. Slaves' lives, and their right thereto, were always viewed from the perspective of the master—as abortion is today, where the pregnant woman can decide what to do with "her fetus." Since slaves were not deemed human, they had no independent right to life, separate from the dictates of their masters. Indeed, masters in some colonies had the virtual right to kill slaves if they felt they had cause to do so. Just as the unborn child today enjoys no legal protection from abortion, so black people under enslavement had no legal rights to their own body. All such rights were retained by the master. One court of law even held that a slave had "no will of his own . . . such obedience (to the master) is the consequence only of uncontrolled authority over the body. There is nothing else that can produce the effect. The power of the master must be absolute to render the submission of the slave perfect."[2]

We see the same power dynamic in current abortion law. The authority of the woman to abort is absolute.[3] And just as today's abortion lobby fights all curbs on abortion, so it was that prior to the Civil War, proponents of slavery vigorously resisted the slightest attempts to curb slavery. The economic reasons for this intransigence are plain. But the obstinacy was fueled by the fear that to permit any restrictions upon slavery, no matter how trivial, would be a tacit admission that: there is something bad, wrong, or undesirable about the institution; such wrongness is a function of the humanity of slaves; and therefore the practice should be abolished entirely. This syllogism holds for today's abortion lobby. The smallest and most modest limitations on the right to an abortion cannot be tolerated, because they might be the first step along the road toward recognizing the humanity of the unborn, and this is verboten as it would lead to a ban on abortion. Hence in the summer of 1996 we have President Clinton vetoing a ban on the grisly partial-birth abortion procedure, wherein all but the head of the baby is delivered, and then the brains of the unborn child are sucked out, thus still killing the child in utero, a "legitimate" abortion.

Denying the essential humanity of blacks and resisting any limitations on the institution of slavery were, alone, insufficient to preserve slavery. To ensure their utter subjugation, attention had to be paid to the slaves themselves. The institution could not long survive unless slaves were rendered as defenseless as an unborn child. So most slave states codified absolute prohibitions against slaves carrying any form of weapon or implement that could be used against their masters. Slaves found in possession of guns, knives, and the like were often subject to severe discipline and beatings. The physical vulnerability of the enslaved was essential to maintain. The abortion rights movement is similarly dependent on the total physical vulnerability of the unborn, a vulnerability that is obviously easy to maintain. If an unborn child had the chance to defend herself, surely she would. The gruesome sonogram images of unborn children desperately attempting to escape the advancing instruments of the abortionist give stark testament to that fact.

The unborn can do nothing to save herself. Like the slave, the unborn child cannot vote, protest, or exercise economic clout to protect her interests. Although the slave could at least possibly escape or revolt, and even rebel—if only on a very small scale—the unborn has not even this small recourse. Instead, the abortion lobby aggressively tries to silence and control advocates of the unborn to reduce their effectiveness in rallying public and legislative opposition to abortion.[4] To accomplish this, abortion proponents use many of the same mechanisms that slavery proponents once used. Laws restricting picketing at abortion clinics limit the ability of pro-lifers to congregate, and RICO (Racketeer-Influenced and Corrupt Organizations) law is used to disrupt pro-life attempts to organize opposition to abortion. Although unlike the proponents of slavery abortion forces cannot pass legislation prohibiting pro-lifers from reading and writing about the subject, they have done a remarkable job (with the help of a sympathetic media) of squelching widespread dissemination of information about the reality of abortion. They realize that if knowledge of the nature of abortion were to become widespread, public revulsion would ensue and abortion practice could well be altered, just as images of Bull Connor's dogs attacking black Southerners during the civil rights movement helped expose to the country the evil of Jim Crow. Anyone who has ever seen photographs of an aborted human being can attest to the horror of these images and the impact they would certainly have on the nation. Dispassionate review of film of the inside of abortion clinics would be virtually impossible. Broadcast of such scenes, a sort of high-tech *Uncle Tom's Cabin*, could ignite a popular revolt against abortion on demand.

CONSEQUENCES

Without question the practice of abortion on demand has brutalized our culture. The thirty million abortions since *Roe v. Wade* have deadened our moral senses and cheapened the value of human life. A major insidiousness of abortion is that there is no scientific method for assessing the harm it has done to society. There is no visible, quantifiable tether between the mammoth abortion rate and the increase in child abuse, spousal abuse, divorce, teen pregnancy, sexual promiscuity, and murder.[5] A correlation between abortion and pathologies running rampant in society is easily dismissed for lack of empirical evidence. Nonetheless, it would seem *prima facie* reasonable to assert a socially negative impact of liberal abortion practice.

Interestingly, the peripheral effects of slavery were similarly difficult to quantify. However, it can be said with reasonable certainty that the residual effects still plague us today. The current economic and social disparities between blacks and whites and the maladies flowing therefrom may in some measure be traced to the impact of slavery. And, of course, some of the direct effects of slavery are well known: the Civil War, post-Reconstruction, Jim Crow, an agrarian southern economy loath to advance or diversify, and others.

We err if we think that black Americans are not negatively impacted by abortion on demand. The abortion rate for blacks is nearly three times the black population, and some on both the Right and the Left are pro-choice out of a racist motivation to keep the number of blacks in the population as low as possible.[6] Today we look back with respect and reverence at those who fought for basic human dignity for blacks. We view those who did not with bewilderment and those who fought against it with disdain. I would like to suggest that how future generations remember us will depend in large part on our resolution of the abortion question and on where we now stand on this issue. If abortion is permitted to continue on the present scale, it is inescapable that hearts will continue to be hardened and future generations will view us as misguided and cowardly. But if abortion is drastically reduced, future generations will view us in the same grateful light that those who fought against slavery are viewed today.

NOTES

1. See, for example, James Davison Hunter, *Before the Shooting Begins: Searching for Democracy in America's Culture Wars* (New York: Free Press, 1994).

2. *State v. Mann*, 13 N. C. 263 (1829), at 266.

3. This is not the norm in most Western nations; see May Ann Glendon, *Abortion and Divorce in Western Law* (Cambridge, Mass.: Harvard University Press, 1987).

4. For discussion of the general cultural reluctance to openly consider the unborn and the violence abortion does to them, see Brad Stetson, ed., *The Silent Subject: Reflections on the Unborn in American Culture* (Westport, Conn.: Praeger, 1996).

5. For a comprehensive description of the psychological and emotional trauma endured by some women who have undergone abortions, see David Reardon, *Aborted Women, Silent No More* (Chicago: Loyola University Press, 1987).

6. On the abortion rate, see the statistics from the Alan Guttmacher Institute, cited in Tom Bethell, "Roe's Disparate Impact," *American Spectator* (June 1996): 18–19. On the racist nature of some support for abortion, see "Buckley: Abortion Backed by Some with Racist Intent," *Orange County Register*, 2 June 1996, News 13. See also Robert Marshall and Charles Donovan, *Blessed Are the Barren: The Social Policy of Planned Parenthood* (San Francisco: Ignatius Press, 1991).

21

IS THIS THE WORK OF GOD?
REFLECTIONS ON THE BLACK CHURCH

Jesse Peterson

Black America holds mainstream social norms, and its leaders know the ravages that drugs, crime and dependency have meant for black areas. Yet black community leaders such as clergymen seldom speak up publicly for enforcing mores.

Lawrence Mead, political economist

One of Los Angeles's most prominent and revered black ministers is combatting AIDS by passing out condoms to his congregants' children. A pair of the city's other leading black clergy have tacitly endorsed the practice by meeting with the first minister and saying nothing to condemn his practice. Another prominent black minister in Maryland allowed President Clinton to use his pulpit to further his own political agenda, even though President Clinton aggressively pushes policies that most black people oppose, especially homosexuality, abortion, and back-breaking taxes. Why are black preachers so out of step with most of the black public?

THE POLITICIZED PULPIT

It wasn't always this way. When I was growing up in the late 1950s and early 1960s, the black church rightly emphasized God and salvation, as well as rebuilding the family with stress on the man as the head of this marriage-based, two-parent family. But today, it seems that many black churches talk less about God and more about race and politics, and the need for activistic government.

There are at least two obvious reasons for this change. The first is that since talking about racial animosity and politics will get a black minister publicity, many have stopped preaching the Gospel and have instead started preaching liberalism. A second reason is the simple fact that many of these men are called to preach by their grandmothers and mothers, not by God. This has led to a hyperemotionalism in many black churches; this emotionalism is counterproductive and dangerous, for it can easily be co-opted by someone who is a powerful orator but whose message is harmful.

All of which has had a corrupting influence in so many black churches. While urban black communities are literally falling apart, ministers are striving to build bigger churches and to maximize the membership of their churches. But Jesus came to give life, not fame and money. We have an out-of-wedlock pregnancy rate of nearly 70 percent—and higher in large cities; blacks make up over half the prison population in this country;[1] random violence terrorizes black neighborhoods; husbands walk out on their wives and families; and drugs are openly sold on the streets. This does not sound like the abundant life promised by the Gospel. With black churches on almost every street corner in black neighborhoods, we have to begin to examine why the church is so ineffective at bringing life to black communities.

In November of 1994 I spoke at a church in Alabama. After I spoke about BOND and the impact it has had on young black men, I began to speak frankly and honestly about problems in many urban black communities: brutal violence, sexual promiscuity, out-of-wedlock pregnancy, anger, and drug abuse. The minister of the church became very uncomfortable. He said we weren't preaching Jesus, and he brought the meeting to a close, showing me the door. Most of the congregation was upset with the minister, because they felt that for the first time they were being told the truth about what hinders black progress in this country. What I was saying made sense to them. But their minister was not interested in this. I commonly receive this reaction when I speak at black churches.

But the fact is, the black family is not going to be restored and black communities are not going to grow stronger until people truly rely on God, not on their ministers or politicians. We need to relearn the meaning of self-responsibility. We need women who will respect their husbands, we need men who will look to God, and we need children who will turn back to their fathers. Then and only then will we begin to see character develop once again within the black family. To my mind, the proper order of life is God, Jesus, man, woman, and children. When that order is broken, the individual and the family will both suffer. Today, we need to remember God's command to the Jewish nation: "Ye shall have no other gods before Me."

NOTE

1. See John J. DiIulio, Jr., "The Coming of the Super-Predators," *Weekly Standard*, 27 November 1995, 23–28, for an analysis of future crime trends in urban, especially black American communities. See also the articles by John J. DiIulio, Jr., "The Question of Black Crime," *Public Interest* no. 117 (fall 1994): 3–56 and "My Black Crime Problem, and Ours," *City Journal* (spring 1996): 14–28.

22

BLACK DIAMONDS: DISCOVERING THE LESSONS OF FREEDOM IN BLACK CONSERVATIVE THOUGHT

Stan Faryna

Freedom is the measure of man's dignity and greatness. Living the freedom sought by individuals and peoples is a great challenge to man's spiritual growth and to the moral vitality of nations. The basic question which we must all face today is the responsible use of freedom in both its personal and social dimensions. Our reflection must turn then to the question of the moral structure of freedom, which is the inner architecture of the culture of freedom.

Freedom is not simply the absence of tyranny or oppression. Nor is freedom a license to do whatever we like. Freedom has an inner "logic" which distinguishes it and ennobles it: Freedom is ordered to the truth and is fulfilled in man's quest for truth and in man's living in the truth. Detached from the truth about the human person, freedom deteriorates into license in the lives of individuals, and in political life, it becomes the caprice of the most powerful. Far from being a limitation upon freedom or a threat to it, reference to the truth about the human person—a truth universally knowable through the moral law written on the hearts of all—is, in fact, the guarantor of freedom's future.

                    Pope John Paul II, Address to the UN General Assembly, 1995

THE QUEST FOR FREEDOM

The dawn of a new millennium is approaching, and all the people of the world look upon it with mixed feelings of apprehension and encouragement.

Mixed with our fear for the future, there is hope for "a new flourishing of the human spirit, mediated through an authentic culture of freedom."[1] If that hope is to prevail, we will need to learn the courage to be. We will find this courage in the rediscovery of the crowning virtues of humanity: faith, hope, and love. These virtues are the premise of responsible activity. This "bread," as Reverend Dr. Martin Luther King, Jr., called the virtues, is nurtured in the conscience of every human person.

It is exactly there in a man's own conscience "where man is alone with God and thus perceives that he is not alone amid the enigmas of existence, for he is surrounded by the love of the Creator."[2] In the knowledge of so profound and immense a love, our fears must melt as we gladly go out to meet the challenge of human freedom. As Americans, we should take heart in this love and meet the challenge of freedom with greater enthusiasm, because the quest for freedom is our heritage and our future.

Americans, I believe, enjoy a special place among all peoples. We are the vanguard of the quest for freedom. The United States of America is a shining light that fuels the hope of the entire human family. The wisdom, sacrifice, and struggle that ennobled American civilization is a treasure in which we take deep pride. Such treasure is attended by a greater responsibility. Not only must we guard this treasure for all, but we must increase it and also be generous with it.

From the timeless biblical stories of the Prodigal Son and the Profitable Servant to Charles Dickens's popular *A Christmas Carol* and also Karol Wojtyla's *The Jeweler's Shop*, we know that riches are pleasing to the human heart when they are radiant with the wisdom of their use for good. The increase of the virtues—those qualities for which we admire heroes and saints—follows not only upon their gift, but also their guarding and their good and generous excercise. Similarly, the freedom for which all peoples long passionately will be found in our own sacrifices and struggles to search out the truth and in living truthfully.

Booker T. Washington—who was born a slave and became a hero, a leader, and a scholar—said over a hundred years ago: "Following in the tracks of the lowly Nazarene, we shall continue to work and wait, till, by the exercise of the higher virtues, by the product of our brains and hands, we make ourselves so important to the American people that we shall compel them to recognize us because of our intrinsic worth."[3] Booker T. Washington's hope, that the intrinsic dignity of the human person would be fully recognized in the black American, is a witness to the ongoing quest for freedom in American history. Similarly, Reverend Dr. King's dream for black Americans to enjoy a fuller share in the life of society reminded Americans that the quest for freedom must be constantly renewed. All over the world, we have witnessed that same longing for freedom. As Pope John Paul II told the United Nations General Assembly in 1995, this is truly one of the distinguishing marks of our time. In America, we have known this quest to be a plow that makes way for seeds that will grow into the heavy fruits of freedom.

Black Americans have increased the treasure that belongs to all Americans. When America became disaffected with the cause for freedom, black Americans reminded the world of the intrinsic dignity of the human person and of the universal right of the individual to participate fully in society as is commensurate with his dignity as a free human being. Again and again, black Americans have renewed America in the wisdom that there is a universality to human nature and experience. As Booker T. Washington wrote long ago, suffering was their school[4]—though it is often difficult for some to see that beyond the pain and humility of that immense suffering lies a store of radiant virtues.

The bold, new voices of black conservatives have become forceful voices for freedom because they draw their wisdom from the treasury of their heritage and the greater treasuries of the nation and humanity. As their voices grow stronger, the old foundations of politics and economics will crumble.

These courageous men and women are reawakening black America's trust in itself as a community of free and acting persons who know themselves to be the children of God. They have inaugurated a new beginning for black Americans by giving public notice of the avaliable and real opportunities for them to participate economically, politically, and socially in the life of American civilization. Indeed, the vision of black conservatives is both profound and powerful. It is the same high moral vision Pope John Paul II commended: "The vision of man as a creature of intelligence and free will, immersed in a mystery which transcends his own being and endowed with the ability to reflect and the ability to choose—and thus capable of wisdom and virtue."[5]

Although this vision is grounded in a certain knowledge of the truth of the human person and human civilization, it has been relentlessly criticized, often ignored, and frequently censored. Perhaps the voices of black conservatives have been so unkindly received because their voices are the antidote to the liberal politics whose unsuccessful attempts to advance black socioeconomic progress devastated the black community. This devastation has been observed in the increased rates of crime, illegitimacy, single-parent families, and welfare dependency among other problems that plague inner cities all across America. These problems, however, are only symptoms of a deeper and more serious wound that is open upon the human heart. That wound is the loss for many of the living bread of faith, hope, and love.

Although liberals did not lack good intentions, the overly enthusiastic engineers of social change had begun to sever black Americans from their deeply rooted religious life. Consequently, many lost pride in themselves as acting persons and in that hard-won freedom that came on the heels of extraordinary sufferings and sacrifices. These are the same social forces that reject truth as well as the intelligibility of human nature and experience. They are the same forces that are often described as the mastermind behind the collapse of American civilization that now threatens us—however much unintended.

Among the early victims of the culture wars were those who, like many black Americans, lived in America's inner cities. Indeed, it is often the suffering whose pains are increased by the zealous humanism of the well-intended such as those who died under the totalitarian regimes of Stalin and Hitler among others. Similarly, poverty and the long experience of wounded dignity made the urban black family vulnerable to the impossible promises of social engineers and the elite crowd of intellectuals of the Left. Several persuasive voices among the black conservatives were former advocates of those failed programs, but the unintended catastrophe that befell the black community came as a wake-up call. For example, the Hoover Institute's Dr. Thomas Sowell is a prominent black conservative. A noted author and economist, Sowell is also a former Marxist.

Just as the neo-conservatives defected from the highest ranks of the intellectual elite, many black conservatives defected from liberal politics. Often, they rediscovered the values of their childhood and the strong faith of their fathers and mothers. Many also discovered for the first time that their vision of freedom was better reflected in the conservative movement. If Republicans had missed the bus during the civil rights movement, at least the neo-conservatives knew how to get to the bus stop. With the increasing presence of neo-conservatives during the 1980s, black conservatives found a new interest in them by a movement that once firmly believed—with the Democratic leadership—that the black membership in liberal politics was a done deal. Still, there was no room at the inn, as Justice Clarence Thomas reminds us.

In their supposed betrayal of the black community by seeking truth and upholding the universality of human beings, black conservatives have become a threat to liberal politics and the culture of death that it perpetuates. Constituted by a moral force fueled by powerful intelligence and high moral character, black conservatives such as Dr. Thomas Sowell, Justice Clarence Thomas, and Dr. Walter Williams have become a symbol of hope that extends beyond the black community.

Just as the nonviolent revolutionaries of 1989 reminded people everywhere, black conservativism is a reminder to Americans "that it is possible for man's historical journey to follow a path which is true to the finest aspirations of the human spirit."[6] Their hope reminds us that America can be the same rising sun on the horizon of human freedom that Ben Franklin saw upon General George Washington's chair at the Continental Congress. In confronting the black establishment backed by the power of rhetoric and terror, black conservatives show us how not to be afraid. They teach us that the search for truth (the same search for which human freedom has been given) is the most worthwhile pursuit—though our path may be obstructed by pride and adversity.

More importantly, the bold lessons of freedom that can be found in black conservative thought are lessons that need to be learned by all Americans. Their insistence on an education for freedom, on the necessity of the common good, and the individual's fulfillment that is found in the possession of virtues (among other things) are black diamonds—though they may be diamonds in the rough. It is these black diamonds, however, that are particularly radiant signs of the time. These black diamonds open our eyes to the work we have ahead and the magnificent rewards that such work will bring.

THE EDUCATION OF THE CITIZENRY

Black conservatives such as Justice Clarence Thomas have noted that the challenge of the new millennium confronts us today. In *Racism or Attitude*, Dr. James Robinson notes that "in Clarence Thomas' emphasis on natural law and the principles of the Declaration, he, too, insists that America stands for a moral project that includes blacks as much as whites."[7] As Americans, we should be glad to find ourselves engaged in so noble a project at the end of a century in which the entire human family has suffered profoundly from the ravages of indifference, politics, and war. Indeed, if this is our project, then, we need to prepare ourselves to meet the challenge of human freedom.

But the exhibits in the newly opened Freedom Park in Virginia are a reminder that the quest for freedom does not belong only to Americans, but to all humanity. Among the exhibits in Freedom Park is the headless statue of Lenin, a statue that had once imposingly stared out across St. Petersburg. Another exhibit includes towering pieces of the Berlin Wall, the wall that once divided a city and the world.

Freedom Park also reminds us that we have a great responsibility because America is the symbol of freedom for the whole world. Like the Statue of Liberty, we must hold freedom high because it is a beacon of hope for other peoples. Just as she holds her book close to her, we must also embrace our best laws, institutions, and noble aspirations with jealous affection. Together, we must build a new civilization that is worthy of the high dignity of the human person—a civilization that will shine out and give light to the world.

Such a civilization is the future to which the Founding Fathers commended us. It is the same vision that inspired Reverend Dr. King's Dream. Such perfection, however, will be found only if we renew our love for freedom and our understanding of it. As Justice Thomas has been known to argue, "dignity and pride of citizenship in America cannot be conferred by affirmative or any government action."[8] Therefore, we will need to educate ourselves and our children. The task ahead is to build a true culture of freedom that can contain the flourishing of the human spirit.

A true education in the ways of freedom will open up new and rich possibilities for the entire human family. Among those possibilities is the fulfillment of the deepest and most noble of qualities in the human person: intellectual, moral, and spiritual virtues. This realization makes urgent our need to reflect on whether or not the education of our children satisfies our highest and most noble expectations. If the education of our children is found to be inadequate, we must rebuild them so that they are worthy of our trust. Certainly, this is an exciting time. As Ezola Foster reminded Americans, parents and community have not enjoyed such participation in their children's education since the old school house days.[9]

Why is the best education that which teaches the pursuit of truth for freedom? The good book tells us why, because only truth will set us free. Less ideally, a good education gives students a comprehensive vision of reality—of God, humans, and the world. Such a comprehensive vision would guide our children well in their living and make upstanding citizens of them. Above all, this is what we ought to wish most for our children because the quest for freedom has expanded the horizon of man's aspiration to goodness and truth. In poetic words, Booker T. Washington noted this same goodness of freedom: "Even the treasures of nature in our South-land, that seem to hide themselves from the hand of man, have felt the inspiring thrill of freedom, and coal and iron and marble have left forth, and where once was the overseer's lash, steam and electricity make go the shop, the factory, and the furnace."[10]

Among the lessons of this century, violence has made us aware that when people are freed from self-control, they gain a spontaneity for viciousness that is more menacing than we can imagine. Classrooms where students are free from self-control, then, cannot be said to be preparing our children for the responsibility of freedom. Instead, they permit children to become brutes that go forth and terrorize the streets with a vicious and unruly egotism. While such classrooms may not be obvious, lowered education standards and relaxed classroom standards are breeding grounds for the attrition of the self-control instilled in the home. Students, if they will be students, must act like students. The classroom that does not reinforce the same self-control so painstakingly taught in the home, therefore, must be corrected.

Furthermore, a true education does not liberate students from respect for institutions and traditions so that their loyalties and affections seek only selfish pursuits. As we know from the nightly news, misplaced loyalties end in violent murders and increased incidents of crime. Again, it may not be obvious that what is taught will lead to these problems. Yet how can we not see there is a danger in the emphasis on readings that inspire suspicion, hatred, and a general mistrust for human society and traditions? Certainly, such subjects form dangerous habits of the mind and prevent the development of the student's proper love for one's country. Such intellectual habits as suspicion, mistrust, and fear will confront the challenges of freedom with violence and suspicion. Certainly, they will fail.

While it is important to teach that freedom, truth, and human dignity must tolerate no tyranny, dark imaginations and fears can lead to great evils. The encouragement of suspicion may also lead to the misplaced hatred of the institutions on which freedom, truth, and human dignity depend so dearly. Although we must all be witnesses to the abuses of human dignity that occur and have occurred, we must teach our children to seek positive solutions that will encourage the universal values of justice, liberty, peace, and solidarity.

Students need to learn how to think and examine propositions, but such examinations need to be led by a pursuit of truth as opposed to hatred. Inspiring a student's motivation to learn through these dark passions can only end badly. Unfortunately, many teachers today mistake suspicion for analysis and hatred for conviction. Of course, these are just a few of the issues that we must confront if we are to renew the social fabric and ensure that the quest for freedom continues after we have passed away.

Finally, our schools need to reaffirm the values that we teach at home. An education that does not encourage and promote the exercise of moral goodness could not be said to be an education at all. Long ago, Booker T. Washington warned the Boston congregation of Trinity Church that a school that did not include moral education was to be avoided.

The study of Arithmetic that does not result in making someone more honest and self-reliant is defective. The study of history that does not result in making men conscientious in receiving and counting the ballots of their fellow men is most faulty. The study of art that does not result in making the strong less willing to oppress the weak, means little.[11]

What sort of education, exactly, should we want to give our children? Christian philosopher Jacques Maritain, an immigrant, recommended that an "education for freedom should be directed to wisdom, centered in the humanities, and developing the capacity to enjoy truth and beauty." Although the home is the most persuasive teacher of our children, the schools to which we send them should give them a more thoughtful appreciation for freedom and its institutions. They should not come home in the afternoon with a lost respect for the country and the laws by which we pursue the quest for freedom together.

THE COMMON GOOD

Although we should trust in the future, there is a need to realize that good future to which we all aspire. As black conservatives often comment, the task requires putting American society and ourselves in order. This is a difficult and dangerous task—for we must deal with crime and violence in ways we have not fully dared before. We will need to revitalize the ethical dimensions of American life, if we are going to renew the quest for freedom.[12] We will also need to learn to love and be responsible.[13]

Do we lock the gangsters and criminals up, and throw away the key? Do we put a police officer on every street corner? Tough sentences are important as George Mason University's Dr. Walter Williams has written. Tough sentencing is not the cure, however, for the breakdown of human civilization. It is not the solution because civilization is not made effective by force. Human society did not arise out of the tyranny of power. Indeed, real authority is neither justified nor made effective by force.[14]

The viewpoint that the criminal cannot be reformed seems to be a misunderstanding of human nature as well as the rejection of redemption. Reverend Steven Craft, a reformed and God-fearing ex-convict, would disagree completely with that viewpoint. Such rejection of the power of change and God's ability to change the human heart is a symptom of the profound unbelief that has spread across the nation in this century.

Since ancient civilization, the law has been understood as an ordinance of reason that was issued by those who have care of the community.[15] Law has also been understood as a rule of reason that directs the actions of people to the "good of the many, and in its fullest dimension: the good of all."[16] It is a view that seems rare today, but the Christian philosopher Yves Simon often emphasized the traditional understanding of the law in contrast to modern misunderstandings. In this century, Simon also agreed that the law should be understood as sustaining "a good unique in plenitude and duration, the common good of the human community."[17]

People are not born perfected in the virtues. In fact, they are completely capable of turning away from the divine law. That turning away from God, however, does not just have a devastating consequence for the individual. It also has devastating impact on the entire human family. Beyond the rejection of salvation, the turning away from the divine law leads to behavior that destroys human relationships. Human laws, however, provide the means by which human society is sustained through a common good.

A just law, for example, causes a unity of action—unity in a firm and stable manner. This is a vital function, as Simon comments: "By the very fact that a community comprises a number of individuals, the unity of its action cannot be taken for granted: it has to be caused. Further, if the community is to endure, the cause of its united action must be firm and stable."[18] Dr. King understood these points with extraordinary grasp.

In fact, Dr. King's viewpoint of law had its origin in St. Thomas Aquinas's treatise on the natural law—a viewpoint for which critics have attacked U.S. Supreme Court Justice Clarence Thomas. Aquinas writes:

Law is a rule and measure of acts whereby the agent is induced to act or is restrained from acting for lex [law] is derived from ligare [to bind], because it binds one to act. Now the rule and measure of human acts is reason, which is the first principle of human acts. . . . It belongs to reason to direct to an end, which is the first principle in all matters of action, according to the Philosopher [Aristotle]. That which is the principle in any genus is the rule and measure of that genus.[19]

If we accept that human law as a principle of human acts, we must admit that the law regards the "ordering to happiness"[20] and the ordering "to the common good."[21]

This character of the law—as directing acts toward a transcendent end—had special significance for Aquinas.[22] All laws decreed in the exercise of right reason, he found, derive from the eternal law. Although human law derives from the eternal law, however, "it is not on a perfect equality with it."[23]

These theological considerations illuminate human law in ways that we will need to think about more. Indeed, these kinds of considerations have been ignored since Hobbes. The viewpoint opens up a deeper meditation on the law. It may also foster greater respect for it, since the law not only makes political society possible, but also lends to the perfection of the individual. Centuries ago, it was recognized that the human law also makes possible the individual's participation in divine reason. Karol Wojtyla explains: "The encounter of human reason in its orientation toward the objective order is an encounter with the divine source of law. This encounter is very profound, for it involves participation in the eternal law, which is in some sense identical with God, with divine reason."[24]

As we have seen in recent times, force neither encourages the culture of freedom nor sustains human civilization. Obviously, coercion fails to make the law effective in the hearts of men. The analysis, however, seems to be turned around and backward. It is human nature that demands civil society for its own completion. This basic need for completion and the human relationships (which arise out of these basic necessities) gives the law authority over people.

In the introduction to Simon's book, *The Tradition of Natural Law*, John Hallowell clarifies this point. He writes that the natural law "asserts that there are certain ways of behaving which are appropriate to man simply by virtue of the fact that he is a human being."[25]

Natural law scholars such as Justice Thomas argue that human law is made effective by our desire and ability to possess right reason—not by force. As Dr. King emphasized, law is also made effective by the source of law, God. If it is not effective, then it must be unjust. The unjust law lacks the divine authority (partially or fully) that is active in just laws.

The relationship between law and God is well illustrated by King in his "Letter from Birmingham City Jail."

How does one determine when a law is just or unjust? A just law is a man-made code that squares with the moral law or law of God. An unjust law is a code that is out of harmony with the moral law. To put it in the terms of Saint Thomas Aquinas, an unjust law is a human law that is not rooted in eternal and natural law.[26]

King's distinction of just and unjust laws is important for us to understand.

But if we are going to love the law and become friends to it, we need to distinguish between just and unjust laws. Otherwise, our friendship with the law will fail to inspire others to seek the same friendship. If we befriend an unjust law, we scandalize the law. Certainly, this is a friendship we need to teach to those disillusioned with the system, such as rapper Ice Cube. We also need to teach this friendship to those who never enjoyed formation into the life of the common good.[27]

PLANTING THE SEEDS OF FREEDOM

Obeying the law will help us be virtuous, but we should not expect to become virtuous by the mere obedience to the law. As Ezola Foster often recommends, we need to plant the seeds of freedom and nurture them through the seasons. There remain the certain need for character and the need to act in order to become good. Thus we all need to pursue virtue because they are a completion of the person.[28] As such, the need to understand the virtues is as important as making them ours. We will not make the virtues our own until we have clearly understood them.

Most people know that virtue is doing what is right. Doing what is right, however, is not so simple. Most people don't realize that virtue is a special habit in choosing what is right over what is wrong. In other words, virtue is about making a good decision about how we will act. But virtue doesn't necessarily happen at once. The pursuit of virtue demands making a good decision again and again.

Just as people who have decided to quit smoking often do not succeed in stopping the first time they try it, so virtue is difficult to achieve. It is possible and the rewards are rich. Virtue teaches us how we shall accomplish good things. The virtues also enable us to live with each other. At least, this is one description of the virtues. Developing further the insights of the Greek philosopher Aristotle, the Roman Catholic Aquinas wrote a great deal about the virtues. He observed, for example, that the human virtues are "good habits, productive of good works."[29] They are good, Aquinas explained, because "all evil implies defect,"[30] and virtue is a perfection.

What are the subjects of virtue? Aquinas says that they are those powers that can be modified by habits. Fortunately, Aquinas spelled them out for us with incredible precision and clarity: the powers of the soul, intellect, appetites, and will. Those habits of the soul that can be perfected are a subject of the theological virtues. Intellectual virtues are those habits that well dispose the intellect through the rectitude of the will. Last but not least, the sensible appetites are able to participate in reason (obey) through habits of reason. These habits are called the moral virtues.

The natural virtues include both the intellectual and moral virtues. Aquinas explained that all virtues originate, increase, and diminish by human activity. In this light, we begin to see more fully how these virtues are all "habits perfecting man in view of his doing good deeds."[31] Moral virtues, however, are habits of the appetitive part. In other words, they affect one as a whole. The intellectual virtues are not dispositions, however, to do that which is good for the whole. As Garrigou-Lagrange comments, "they fail to make one morally good."[32]

This distinction between the intellectual and moral virtues is well illustrated in comparing the virtues of art and prudence. Art is *ratio factibilium*, which means "to make something outside man," whereas prudence is *recta ratio agibilium*, which means "to do something that remains inside." Nonetheless, although the habits that perfect the intellect and those that perfect our appetitive part are not the same, they are related. Indeed, you cannot have moral virtue without certain intellectual virtues. Aquinas points out this unity of the virtues in Question 58 of his *Summa Theologica*: "Accordingly for a man to do a good deed, it is requisite not only that his reason be well disposed by means of a habit of intellectual virtue; but also that his appetite be well disposed by means of a moral virtue."[33]

What are the intellectual virtues? The intellectual virtues are five: science, wisdom, understanding, prudence, and art. All are directed to good ends theoretically rather than the good end of the human person. In other words, the intellectual virtues dispose us to a good activity like science, but not necessarily to good action. The intellectual virtues constitute the perfection of the speculative and practical intellect of the human person.

The will, then, is subordinated to the particular end of an intellectual virtue. At the same time, the will must integrate the particular ends of the intellectual virtue with the general end of the human person. Aquinas distinguishes two categories among the intellectual virtues: those that presuppose a certain goodwill and those that do not presuppose a certain goodwill. Prudence, for example, is of the former group; science and art are of the latter.

The moral virtues are habits of the appetitive part. They "imply rectitude of the appetite [and] are called principal virtues"[34] (including the one intellectual-moral virtue: prudence). Furthermore, "Prudence is the principle of all the virtues simply. The others are principal, each in its own genus."[35] Thomas also referred to the principal virtues as the cardinal virtues whose goods are defined by reason:

First, as existing in the very act of reason: and thus we have one principal virtue, called Prudence. Secondly, according as the reason puts its order into something else; either into operations, and then we have Justice; or into passions, and then we need two virtues. For the need of putting the order of reason into the passions is due to thwarting reason; and then the passions need a curb, which we call Temperance. Secondly, by the passions withdrawing us from following the dictate of reason, e.g., through fear of danger or toil: and then man needs to be strengthened for that which reason dictates, lest he turn back; and to this end there is Fortitude.[36]

The four cardinal virtues can be distinguished in two ways: as general virtues and special virtues. As general virtues, they are understood in their common formal principles. Aquinas gave the following example: "every virtue that causes the good of right and due in operations"[37] can be called justice. But as special virtues, they "may be considered in point of their being denominated, each one from that which is foremost in its respective matter."[38] Aquinas illustrated the cardinal virtues as special virtues in the following way: "so that prudence is the virtue which commands; justice, the virtue which is about due actions between equals; temperance, the virtue that suppresses desires for the pleasures of touch; and fortitude, the virtue which strengthens against dangers of death."[39]

In Question 62 of his *Summa Theologica*, Aquinas said that "Man is perfected by virtue, for those actions whereby he is directed to happiness."[40] He further explained that human happiness is twofold. "One is proportionate to human nature."[41] This happiness is obtained by natural principles (right reason); the other happiness surpasses human nature. It cannot be attained only by the power of God.

Aquinas described how this power of God is a "kind of participation of the Godhead,"[42] in which the human person receives divine principles that are incomprehensible to human reason. Unlike the natural virtues, these divine principles are not found in right reason. Nor do these principles well-dispose one to natural ends. Instead, these principles dispose Christians to live in a special relationship with the Holy Trinity. Indeed, the Church teaches that they are the foundation and animating spirit of Christian moral action. They are that which makes it possible for the person to be good.

Of course, these principles are the articles of faith, hope, and charity. King had referred to these when speaking about the three loaves of bread: the bread of faith, the bread of hope, and the bread of charity.[43] As the church teaches, all of these special virtues are infused into the souls of the faithful. Moreover, the articles of faith are principles by which the intellect is directed to God, the articles of hope are principles that order the will to God, and the articles of charity have a twofold task: they both move and conform the appetites to God.[44] In light of these articles, we can see how the Christian life of grace consists in the exercise and cultivation of these theological virtues. It is no wonder, then, that black conservatives often recommend them.

Faith is the disposition to believe in God, in what He has taught about Himself, and about our relation to Him. "Hence, the mean on which faith is based is the Divine Truth."[45] It is also a mean between science and opinion. As an act, Aquinas describes faith as having "something in common with science and understanding; yet its knowledge does not attain the perfection of clear sight."[46] Instead, the perfection of this supernatural habit is in the act of living faith in the assent to the first truth (Belief of God) and other divine truths. Faith is also the trusting in these truths.

Hope is the disposition of expecting that eternal life with God. This eternal life has been promised to us, and it can be attained despite the difficulties involved. It is attainable exactly because God allows us and helps us attain it. It this regard, hope is a movement of the appetitive faculty to eternal happiness. Hope regards this chiefly and other things, secondarily. Moreover, it is a habit that resides in the will. Aquinas explained that a living hope "makes us adhere to God as the source whence we derive perfect goodness, i.e., in so far as, by hope, we trust to the divine assistance for obtaining happiness."[47] Indeed, it is hope that responds to the human aspiration for happiness; it takes up the hopes that inspire men's activities and purifies them so as to order them to the Kingdom of Heaven.

Charity is love for God with the kind of friendship that is made possible by the incarnation and love of other people in imitation of the love Christ has for them. It is the virtue by which we love God above all things for His own sake and our neighbors as ourselves for the love of God. Charity is a virtue by unity of the Divine Goodness, and it is the virtue that attains God most. In other words, charity is superior to all the virtues; it is the greatest of the theological virtues. Charity is the form of the virtues, articulating and ordering them among themselves. It upholds and purifies our human ability to love, it raises the human ability to love to the theological perfection of divine love, and it is the source and goal of Christian practice.

Although the theological virtues are received in the order of faith, hope, and charity, the order of perfection is exactly opposite. Charity is followed by hope, and hope is followed by faith. Aquinas also observed that "charity is the mother and root of all the virtues, inasmuch as it is the form of them all."[48] These are important distinctions about the natural and theological virtues; these distinctions reveal far more than the structure of the virtues but also the manner in which human fulfillment may be rewardingly pursued. The differences between the natural and theological virtues illuminate the full reality in which the human person exists. The congruencies between the natural and theological virtues illuminate how man is a unity and not divided by two different and contradicting realities.

As Reverend Dr. King, Jr., noted long ago, these are important things to understand and can help us live our lives more authentically. Certainly, the challenge of freedom demands the exercise of the several virtues. In understanding the virtues, then, we will find that the quest of freedom can be a realistic endeavor. In fact, virtue is something we should be teaching in our homes and our schools and not just in our churches and temples.

NOTES

1. Pope John Paul II, "The Fabric of Nations: 10/5/95 Address to U.N. General Assembly." Washington, D.C., Origins, CNS Documentary Service 25, no. 18 (October 19, 1995): 299.

2. Ibid.

3. Booker T. Washington, *Black Diamonds: The Wisdom of Booker T. Washington*, Selected and arranged by Victoria Earle Matthews (Deerfield Beach, Fla.: Health Communications, 1995), 105.

4. Booker T. Washington, *Up from Slavery* (New York: Oxford University Press, 1995), 174.

5. Pope John Paul II, "The Fabric of Nations," 295.

6. Ibid.

7. James L. Robinson, *Racism or Attitude: The Ongoing Struggle for Black Liberation and Self Esteem* (New York: Insight Books: 1995), 181.

8. Ibid., 182.

9. Ezola Foster, "Vision, Virtue, Vigilance—America's Survival Kit," *Headway*, January 1996, 29.

10. Washington, *Black Diamonds*, 148.

11. Ibid., 151.

12. See Claes Ryn's *Democracy and the Ethical Life: A Philosophy of Politics and Community* (Washington, D.C.: Catholic University of America Press, 1990). Also see Yves Simon's *Philosophy of Democratic Government* (Chicago: University of Chicago Press, 1980).

13. See Karol Wojtyla's book, *Love & Responsibility* (New York: Farrar, Straus and Giroux, 1981). Also see his book, *Jeweler's Shop* (San Francisco: Ignatius, 1980).

14. Yves Simon illuminates the nature of authority in his *A General Theory of Authority* (Notre Dame, Ind.: University of Notre Dame Press, 1980).

15. Karol Wojtyla, *Person and Community: Selected Essays*, Theresa Sandok, O.S.M., trans. (New York: Peter Lang, 1993), 183.

16. Ibid., 249.

17. Yves R. Simon, *The Tradition of Natural Law: A Philosopher's Reflections* (New York: Fordham University Press, 1992), 29.

18. Simon, *A General Theory of Authority*, 32.

19. Saint Thomas Aquinas, *De Legibus*, Russell Hittinger, transl., ST I-II 90. 1. A more accessible translation of key passages in Aquinas's treatment of natural law is William P. Baumgarth and Richard Regan, S.J., eds., *Saint Thomas Aquinas: On Law, Morality, and Politics* (Indianapolis, Ind.: Hackett, 1988).

20. Ibid., I-II 90. 2. The first principle of natural law is to do good and avoid evil. For a treatment of the principles of the natural law, see Ross A. Armstrong, *Primary and Secondary Precepts in Thomistic Natural Law Teaching* (The Hague: Nijhoff, 1966).

21. Ibid., I-II 90. 3.

22. A wonderful and very readable account of the life of St. Thomas Aquinas is G. K. Chesterton's *St. Thomas Aquinas* (Garden City, N.Y.: Image Books, 1956).

23. Aquinas, *De Legibus*, I-II 93. 3.

24. Wojtyla, *Person and Community: Selected Essays*, 184.

25. John H. Hallowell, "Foreword" in Simon, *The Tradition of Natural Law: A Philosopher's Reflections*, viii.

26. James Melvin Washington, ed., "Letter from Birmingham City Jail." *The Strength to Love: A Testament of Hope: The Essential Writings and Speeches of Martin Luther King, Jr.* (San Francisco: Harper, 1986), 293.

27. An excellent description of the philosophy of St. Thomas Aquinas is Etienne Gilson's *The Christian Philosophy of St. Thomas Aquinas* (New York: Random House, 1956). Another good description is Josef Pieper's *Guide to Thomas Aquinas* (New York: Pantheon Books, 1962).

28. A general treatment of the virtues is Simon Harak's *Virtuous Passions: The Formation of Christian Character* (New York: Paulist Press, 1993). A more illuminating work is Ralph McInerny's *Aquinas on Human Action* (Washington, D.C.: Catholic University of America Press, 1992).

29. St. Thomas Aquinas, *Summa Theologica*, Volume Two, Fathers of the English Dominican Province, translators (Westminster, Md.: Christian Classics, 1981), I-II 55. 3.

30. Ibid.

31. Ibid., 58. 3.

32. R. Garrigou-Lagrange, *The Theological Virtues*, Volume 1 (St. Louis, Mo.: B. Herder, 1965), xii.

33. *Summa Theologica*, I-II 58. 2.

34. Ibid., 61.1. Also see Josef Pieper's *The Four Cardinal Virtues: Prudence, Justice, Fortitude, and Temperance* (New York: Harcourt, Brace, and World, 1965).

35. *Summa Theologica*, 61. 2.

36. Ibid., 60. 2.

37. Ibid., 60. 3.

38. Ibid.

39. Ibid.

40. Ibid., 62. 1.

41. Ibid.

42. Ibid.

43. Washington, *The Strength to Love*, 499.

44. *Summa Theologica*, 62. 3.

45. Ibid., II-II 1. 1.
46. Ibid., 2. 1.
47. Ibid., 17. 6.
48. Ibid., I-II 62. 4.

V

PERSPECTIVES
ON AMERICA

This final section features original conversations with three high-profile black dissidents. Presented in interview form rather than as essays, these dialogues—which were unscripted and extemporaneous—offer a flavor of the public language of black conservative discourse and illustrate the broad range of national concern characteristic of black conservatism. The overarching theme of these interviews is America and the viability of the American project for black advancement. Each of these interviewees refreshingly—and tenaciously—defends mainstream American norms and the efficacy of the work ethic as a means to self-promotion.

In Chapter 23, bestselling author Shelby Steele addresses American political culture and the democratic experiment, seeing in it the potential for genuine national community. Chapter 24 presents the common-sense honesty of Ezola Foster and her unabashed confidence in traditional values as a solution to America's social turmoil. Lastly, in Chapter 25, Larry Elder articulates the elements of a libertarian critique of America's racial obsession and enmity.

Altogether, these conversations are a fascinating and inspiring affirmation of the United States as an experiment in ordered liberty and self-government.

23

A CONVERSATION WITH SHELBY STEELE

Joseph G. Conti and Brad Stetson

CONTI and STETSON: Shelby, what are your current impressions about the state and direction of dissident black social criticism in this country today?[1]

STEELE: Well, the rising voices of black dissent on racial politics really are an irrepressible force. They are meeting a void produced from the other side, because all we are getting from the more traditional civil rights leadership is an ideology that is now approaching half-a-century in age, and is just not speaking to the situation that American blacks are in today. In terms of ideas and insights, the great advantage that the dissidents—who themselves speak from a variety of perspectives—have is that they are intellectually vigorous; they are not tied to a single agenda. So they are increasing in influence, and this will continue.

C & S: Do you think that this increasing influence of black dissidents is reflected in Colin Powell's recent explicit affiliation with the Republican party, an affiliation that Jesse Jackson called "a step backward"?[2]

STEELE: I would say the opposite, it's a step forward, and it reflects a confidence on Powell's part that he could do that and still garner a considerable black vote. Powell said—in what a friend of mine called his "Great Refusal"—that he hoped to expand the Republican party, to diversify it, and I think he is capable of doing that.

C & S: Do you see Powell as a unifying figure?

STEELE: I do, I think he is a unifying figure. What he will do in the future I don't know; this did seem to be his moment. History had aligned itself in a way that it rarely does for anybody, and sort of just asked him to step forward, and he refused. Whether he will step forward again in 2000, no one knows.

C & S: Well, we saw his press conference and thought he was very impressive. Indeed, it even seems as though his stature as a result of his refusal will increase, since, unlike so many potential candidates, getting elected to office did not seem to be his top priority in life.

STEELE: Yes, I've heard that reaction. In fact, I've been a little surprised at how well he's been treated. I thought people might say, "He backed down." But that will be the debate about him, whether this was a sign of character or cowardice.

C & S: Do you think Powell's candidacy would have been a challenge to those black voters who are superficially liberal politically, but deeper down are generally conservative in their social values? Do you think it might have compelled them to reexamine their liberal identity?

STEELE: Absolutely. I have many liberal black friends, and my feeling is that Colin Powell more than anyone else on the scene right now would have challenged the victim-focused political realities that liberal blacks have subscribed to for so long now. He would have made inroads into that form of politics. More than anything else, that's why I'm sad to see him leave the scene as a candidate, because I think in terms of black Americans that is where he would have made a significant contribution.

C & S: So his candidacy would not have been simply a preaching to the choir when it came to blacks; he would not have been simply collecting the votes automatically, but it would have provoked in some cases a revolution in thinking among people who would not be amenable to Powell's ideas if they came from other sources.

STEELE: It would have been a quiet revolution. I think the liberal black friends I have would have voted for Colin Powell, once they got in that booth and they had a chance for the first time in American history to vote for a black man. But then if he would have gotten into office, they would have had to examine themselves, and see if they voted for him just because he was black, or whether there were also some things that he stood for that they liked. There is a lot about Powell that black people were impressed with: his dignity, the dignity of his family, and the positive image of the black family he presented, especially since so much of the propaganda today is otherwise. Along with these things, as time went on I think, a lot of people would have reevaluated their politics.

C & S: Is there a struggle going on for the political hearts of black Americans, a struggle between the juxtaposed figures of Colin Powell and Louis Farrakhan? Powell, on the one hand, affirming the American project—standing with Martin Luther King and saying, "I refuse to believe the bank of justice is bankrupt"—and, Farrakhan, on the other hand, emphasizing race and responsible masculinity (although, of course, with Farrakhan this message is mixed in with a vitriolic hatred and assorted bizarre notions). Do you see such a conflict developing between the Powell style and the Farrakhan style, do you see Farrakhan's influence snowballing in the wake of the Million Man March?³

STEELE: Actually, I don't see it that way at all. I think Farrakhan will go up in smoke. He is not politically sophisticated, he has never been able to successfully manage an organization of any kind, and I just don't think he has the skills required to exploit the momentum of the Million Man March. I think he is going to remain what he is, at best, and that he will not be able to become a major player in the political arena. He is overrated.

C & S: We both thought it was perverse and yet so telling when the day after the Million Man March he held a press conference to assert that the alleged undercount of the march attendance was the result of a racist plot.

STEELE: Well, he's just Louis Farrakhan. You know, I think people just wanted to march, and make a public testament that black males are under siege, and feeling badly about their situation, with such high rates of criminal involvement. People legitimately wanted to make an expression of concern. It's just a tragedy that Louis Farrakhan was the one to exploit that sentiment. Roy Innis put it very well, when he said that Farrakhan had exploited the very sincere and honest aspirations of black men. Again, this just underlines my disappointment at the decision of Colin Powell not to run. Aside from my feelings about his politics one way or the other, as a symbolic figure he was certainly more healthy and forward looking than Louis Farrakhan. Powell said the right things and stood for the right things, and, even if, for example, he were to be secretary of state, I don't know if he'll be able to play that same symbolic role and make that same contribution.

C & S: What about your present work at the Hoover Institution; is some of it related to any of the principles and dynamics you've just alluded to?

STEELE: Well, I'm thinking a lot right now about the very idea of principles, and democratic principles specifically, as opposed to what I call for lack of a better phrase the atavism of race, ethnicity, and gender, these irrational forces that have received so much attention the last few decades and have become more of a source of identity for Americans than our citizenship and our ideas. That seems to me to be a fundamental tension today, and Powell is a good example of someone who is a citizen and an American first, before he is black, before that atavism is given credence, and I think that is the way it should be, and the only proportion for us as Americans to encourage. Farrakhan, as an example, is the opposite of this. The ethnic atavism is all, race is everything, and that's a tragic approach in my view, a blind alley.

C & S: You've written about the emptiness and formality of race as a category, and the dangers associated with that.[4] You've also spoken about the left's incoherent understanding of phrases they generate, like "multiculturalism," for example. What do you see as incoherent about multiculturalism?

STEELE: Well, I see it as virtue without principle. By that I mean that "diversity," "multiculturalism," this language of virtue, lacks principle. In fact, principle becomes demonized; it is seen as oppressive and difficult, and at odds with these amorphous "virtues" like diversity. I see this as incoherence, because without principle, virtues mean nothing. Where's the discipline, hard work, and sacrifice? That comes from principle. That doesn't come from just naming a vague virtue like "diversity."

C & S: Yes, isn't it true that many of these words that are so prominent today, like "diversity" and "multiculturalism" are sort of like puppets, empty figures in which an agenda of leftism is inserted, and in the name of "diversity" pursued?

STEELE: Yes, behind it is some power, somewhere. When a corporation says, "We have a new diversity program," they may not be necessarily grabbing new power, but they are certainly maintaining power, that is, their situation or position. So there is always a corruption when there is no principle that grounds virtue.

C & S: Does contemporary liberalism have the intellectual substance to supply this kind of principle?

STEELE: No, I don't think it does, because it gave up principles; it threw principles in to the lap of the right. So the right ascended intellectually, and the left declined. The left became, in many ways, mere justifiers. Affirmative action, for example, is "justified"; you can't support it by principle. It is a violation of principle. We see this on the left in general, particularly in the universities, with deconstruction and the like. It's all "justification," slick smooth and clever ways of explanation, without recourse to moral principle.

C & S: What is their motivation for taking this approach?

STEELE: Well, I think the motivation was the enormous shame that fell upon the nation as a result of the victorious civil rights movement. America, for the first time, had to face what its history had been like. My feeling is that this shame has been one of the most underrated forces in social policy. It gave whites a mandate, it gave blacks a mandate. For whites, the mandate was redemption. "You must redeem this society form the shame of slavery, segregation, and so forth. You will never have moral authority again until that shame has been redeemed." Of course, one of the reasons we are in the condition we are in today is that our leaders generally don't have the moral authority to enforce democracy and its principles. They are without moral authority. President Clinton has to give a speech and "justify" affirmative action, justify leaving such a policy in place in order to redeem the nation from shame. That is where liberalism got lost. In meeting this mandate for redemption, this hunger for redemption, it made virtue easy; it moved all principle for virtue and practiced expediency. "We'll just have racial preferences," they said, and "we'll just engineer our way to redemption, have a postcard of diversity, and we will be redeemed and have our moral authority back." So I see that as the motivation, but it is so empty of moral principle that it became a corruption.

C & S: Indeed, it seems like we see this very dynamic in President Clinton's Jesse Jackson-esque rhyming defense of affirmative action, "Mend it, don't end it."

STEELE: Yes, it is an unprincipled remark.

C & S: It is a kind of Democratic capitulation to, in this case, the race lobby, and the feminist lobby as well—all of what you called, in an earlier Harper's *article "grievance groups," with their own sovereignties over issues and outrages.[5]*

STEELE: Yes.

C & S: Let us ask you, Shelby, a far more pedestrian question—about the Simpson verdict. One of the racial angles of this event was the ecstatic reaction of many black Americans. What was your own reaction to the rapturous joy of the law students at Howard University when they heard the verdict announced?

STEELE: My feeling is that in this trial there were sort of two moral systems at work. One was what we all identify with, the trial by jury system, where a man is to be judged by a jury of his peers, strictly and objectively on evidence presented at trial. Hovering always above that system was another one, which I call "talionic" for lack of a better word, in the sense of revenge. Talionic impulses are, for example, what is going on in Bosnia. Revenge becomes the predominant force. In this talionic morality, whites and blacks are at odds. Whites were the victimizers, blacks the victims; now blacks are wanting revenge. Their victimization makes them innocent; whites, the victimizers, are guilty—so this was the moral system that was working in that trial. It is, in essence, the race card. That's what Johnnie Cochran, Jr., was so good at. He pulled down this talionic moral system and laid it over the events of the crime. Interestingly, if you pull this down, and you cover the crime with it, O. J. Simpson then becomes the victim. The real victims are utterly forgotten, and Simpson becomes a victim of history. In Cochran's closing remarks, he told the jury "You must do justice." But it wasn't justice by Nicole Brown Simpson and Ron Goldman, but justice by O. J. Simpson, who is a victim of history. He switched victims. That is the race card. It is pulled down to switch victims. But in terms of the students at Howard and other places, the talionic moral system divides us up into teams. I'm on this team of historical victims, and you're on this team of historical victimizers, and my team won.

C & S: It really is the essence of barbarism. My team is everyone who has the color of my skin, your team is everyone who has the color of your skin. It is almost infantile.

STEELE: It is primal. It's atavistic. The shocking thing in the trial was to see how thoroughly the talionic moral system replaced the civic moral system we all depend on as citizens of this nation. Along with this was the tragic irony of Mark Fuhrman, who seemed to be the living, breathing incarnation of the historical victimization of blacks. He had opportunities to tamper with evidence, and Johnnie Cochran, Jr., knew that his strategy would be to call the prosecution's case into question, and Fuhrman would do it, and do it in such a way that it would be difficult not to see reasonable doubt.

C & S: Well, do you think that those who expressed doubt that the predominantly black jury of the Simpson could adjudicate the case fairly had a point?

STEELE: I think this jury received a bad rap. Most of the people I talked to several months before the trial, white and black, thought that there was a reasonable doubt. He's probably guilty as hell, they thought, but still, there's room for reasonable doubt. Well, months later, that pervasive sense is going to have an impact on how the jury viewed the case. They too, like everyone, were caught in this larger drama of history. Then whites became, in a sense, talionic. "Well," they said, "if you put all blacks on this jury, they will never convict." I think that sentiment is false. I think that, as most prosecutors and defense attorneys know, it happens every day. In this case, I think a reasonable person can understand that reasonable doubt was at work. Whether or not I would have voted the same way, I don't know. I certainly would have taken more than four hours to decide, that's unforgivable, and they deserve to be rapped for that. They should have struggled more to reach their decision. But reasonable doubt was a reasonable conclusion, it seems to me, in that case.

C & S: Your work, as a whole, has emphasized psychological aspects of race and race relations. As you look at race relations today, what frame of mind and general attitude do you think people should adopt as they think about race and racial politics?

STEELE: Well, simply, I think people should try to put themselves in the place of the other. We often hear whites say "I can't imagine what it would be like to be black!", but I think that's just silly. We are not talking rocket science, here. We are talking about imagining if one was of a particular race— and knowing what we all know about how that race is generally perceived— what would it be like? It is a matter of empathy. Sometimes we resist that, but when we enter into that we learn things about others and ourselves that we didn't understand before. Of course, what militates against this is that it is usually to my disadvantage. In this politics that we have, it is to my advantage not to know what life is like for you.

C & S: That seems like a strongly humanistic perspective, one that affirms the commonality of people, the ability of a person to transcend her own natural egoism and self-regarding nature.

STEELE: Yes, that's right.

C & S: Finally Shelby, what are your initial general impressions of the newly released book by Dinesh D'Souza, The End of Racism?[6]

STEELE: Well, I don't have a problem with his asserting the possibility of the end of racism, but I do have a problem with what I see as his political usage of the idea. It strikes me that he is using the phrase "the end of racism" in a way that I cannot be respectful of. He is using it to justify a politics and particular set of social and political policies, rather than objectively describing for us how racism might end. In my view, racism will never end any more than lust will, or greed or gluttony or sloth. It is something we will always have to monitor.

C & S: As you know, the book has been a source of deep controversy and division in many circles, including among black conservatives and other dissident thinkers.[7] Yet, people on both sides of the controversy over the book seem to be people of goodwill. They are not opposed to one another on fundamental moral grounds. What has been your reaction to this split?

STEELE: I think it's unfortunate, and I think it's a misunderstanding. I did myself submit a statement at a press conference held by Glenn Loury and

Robert Woodson after the book's release, at which they resigned from the American Enterprise Institute board. I wasn't on the board, so I didn't resign, but I did submit a statement simply making the point that Dinesh D'Souza had every right to write whatever he wished, and I support that right to the bitter end. But just as liberals got into trouble by hiding behind their good intentions—if something was well intended, then it was a justified pursuit—the danger it seems to me for conservatives is hiding behind the First Amendment and the idea of free inquiry. We saw this with the Murray book as well.[8] We were arguing over whether Murray had the right to do the book. Of course he did, but we didn't bother to actually look at the book, and we didn't critically look at his conclusions, like, for example, the conclusion that we should be happy to live in intellectual clans. And D'Souza suggests we should eliminate the 1964 civil rights bill in the private sector. Is this where American conservatism wants to go? These issues, it seems to me, are not being debated, and the two sides of this split are, as you say, good and well-intentioned people who have similar objectives in many ways, and ought to just sit down and talk it over, and see if they can move closer together in their perspectives.

C & S: Thank you.

STEELE: Thank you.

NOTES

This chapter is based on a conversation with Shelby Steele held November 10, 1995, in Monterey, California.

1. Steele's philosophy of race is comprehensively presented in his 1990 bestseller, *The Content of Our Character: A New Vision of Race in America* (New York: St. Martin's Press, 1990), and in his latest book, *The End of Oppression* (New York: HarperCollins, 1996). For interpretive commentary on Steele's work, see Joseph G. Conti and Brad Stetson, *Challenging the Civil Rights Establishment: Profiles of a New Black Vanguard* (Westport, Conn.: Praeger Publishers, 1993), 123–156.

2. For a brief discussion of the growing affinity for the Republican party many blacks today are feeling, see Deroy Murdock, "Black and Right," *National Review*, 11 December 1995, 72. For a representative discussion of the intolerance and hostility that greets many blacks who dissent from the official ideology of mainstream black "leadership," see the remarks by Clarence Thomas, "Confronting the New Intolerance," in the important black conservative periodical, *Issues and Views* (spring 1993):1.

3. For chilling parallels between Farrakhan's Million Man March and the 1934 Nazi party rally in the German city of Nuremburg, see Peter L. Berger, "The 1934 Million Man March," *First Things* (February 1996): 16–17.

4. See, for example, Shelby Steele, "As a Means, Race Always Corrupts in the End," *Orange County Register,* 26 October 1995, Metro 9, and Shelby Steele, "How Liberals Lost Their Virtue over Race," *Newsweek,* 9 January 1995, 41–42.

5. See Shelby Steele, "The New Sovereignties," *Harper's,* July 1992.

6. Dinesh D'Souza, *The End of Racism* (New York: Free Press, 1995).

7. Some black conservatives notable in their public support of D'Souza's book have been Thomas Sowell, Emannuel McLittle, and Elizabeth Wright. See, for example, McLittle and Wright's letter to the *Wall Street Journal,* co-signed by neo-liberal Michael Myers, in *Wall Street Journal,* 20 October 1995, A23. Those black conservatives most notable in their strong criticism of D'Souza's book have been Glenn Loury and Robert Woodson. For their perspective, see Glenn Loury, "A Well-Funded Entry in the Black Inferiority Sweepstakes," *Los Angeles Times,* 24 September 1995, M5. See also Loury's review of *The End of Racism* in the 25 September 1995 edition of *Weekly Standard* magazine. D'Souza's rebuttal to Loury's review is found in *Weekly Standard,* 2 October 1995, 4–5. For general descriptions of the sometimes acrimonious controversy over *The End of Racism,* see "The Fate of Racism," in *U.S. News & World Report,* 18 September 1995, 93–96; "2 Black Conservatives Are Now Searching for a New Home," *Wall Street Journal,* 19 October 1995, A1; and Hugh Pearson, "The End of Racism or Just Its Validation?" *Wall Street Journal,* 5 October 1995, A14. See also the reviews and discussion of *End of Racism* in *The World and I* (January 1996): 245–270. For D'Souza's response to common criticisms of his book, see his extended interview with writer Nicholas Lemann in *American Heritage* magazine, March 1996.

8. Richard J. Herrnstein and Charles Murray, *The Bell Curve: Intelligence and Class Structure in American Life* (New York: Free Press, 1994).

24

AN INTERVIEW WITH EZOLA FOSTER

Joseph G. Conti

CONTI: From your perspective as a black conservative, what is right with America today—and what is wrong?

FOSTER: Your question parallels my book, *What's Right for All Americans!* First, what is wrong with America today? Leadership! From the White House on down to local governments, immoral and indecent and decadent acts have been proselytized and legalized. What's so right about America today? Morality is making a comeback! The American people demanded it with our conservative victory in November of 1994. I believe the people will overcome the powers that be and again have their voices heard in November 1996.

CONTI: Ezola, who decisively influenced and shaped your thinking about race issues—or do you view yourself as largely self-educated in these matters? Can you point to a specific, defining moment in the development of your philosophy on race in America—perhaps an experience?

FOSTER: A high school teacher of mine gave us a lecture on how "that white man" Abraham Lincoln really "didn't care about us Negroes" but that "as the president" he just freed slaves because it was the "political thing" to do. Although I did not challenge her, I had read that Lincoln had come to the realization that slavery was wrong, freed his slaves, and then, as senator from Illinois, went around the country preaching against slavery. It also stayed in my memory how the NAACP had fought so hard to integrate schools and universities. In the city where I grew up, the white school (University of Houston) was situated so close to the black school that the Texas State Legislature suggested the two schools merge. "Oh no," protested the NAACP, "we want our black schools." In my mind, segregation is segregation, be it all-black or all-white. I entered the school not long after it went from being Texas State College for Negroes to Texas Southern University. Combined with these youthful experiences, the "defining moment" actually happened (though I did not know it then) on a sunny Southern California morning in September 1968. That day, I accepted my teaching assignment at David Starr Jordan High School in Watts. This school is rich in "black history": It was the school that started busing in Los Angeles (the 1963 Crawford case).

Following the 1965 Watts Riots and the passage of the 1965 Elementary and Secondary Education Act, it was the school that was used as a blueprint for government funding for "special" (serving nonwhites) school programs. It is a school in a community in which (for a long period of time) all the elected public officials were not only black but also powerful. Among them were State House Speaker Willie Brown, State Assembly Maxine Waters, Congressman Gus Hawkins, State Senators Leroy Green and Diane Watson, former Los Angeles Mayor Tom Bradley, and former Council Representative Gilbert Lindsey.

State House Speaker Willie Brown was said to have been even more powerful than the sitting governor. State Assembly (now Congressional Representative) Maxine Waters has been proclaimed by *Ebony* magazine as the most powerful black woman in America. Of course, Council Representative Gilbert Lindsey was then known as "The Emperor." It was under this leadership that Watts and south central Los Angeles have been researched and reported as "The Killing Fields," "The War Zone," "Beirut, USA." And I was in the midst of it all.

CONTI: Surely the evidence you adduce tends to falsify a key hypothesis of the Left—namely, that problems in black neighborhoods are essentially political. Since these problems are caused by the indifference (or racism) of elected officials, the argument goes, their remedy lies in the election of black liberals to office. This scheme has patently failed in Watts, as you compellingly point out.

You have challenged quite a few conclusions of the Left regarding race relations in America. Has that had any effect on the treatment you receive in local and national media? For instance, do you find that reporters typically play hardball with you and softball with liberals, white and black?

FOSTER: During public policy debates, I am always outnumbered two to one. There are some interviews I consider fair. For instance, Mary Tillotson of "CNN & Co." I thought Charles Grodin was fair during his interview with me and two staunch liberals (black) on race relations. While I enjoy being on the "Larry King Show," it is sometimes, to use his words, "frustrating," to find myself having to take on the host and the guest(s).

With regard to print media, the *Los Angeles Times* has an extremely biased slant toward socialist political movements. For example, following a *Times* story that Mexicans had attacked blacks throughout Los Angeles County jails, a press conference was held on the issue. Included in the media there at the Federal Building press conference were a *Times* reporter and a *Times* photographer. My organization, Americans for Family Values (formerly Black Americans for Family Values), and Jesse Peterson's Brotherhood Organization of New Destiny (BOND) called for the leadership who claim to speak for black Americans (NAACP, Urban League, Southern Christian Leadership, Jesse Jackson, and Maxine Waters) to join us in demanding that illegals (reported as 20% of the jail population) be deported.

May I point out here that this is not the first time that black prisoners have been attacked and severely injured by the so-called Mexican Mafia. As reported, each time, the attacks are planned. Last year, like this one, was at Super Bowl time. While black inmates were watching the game, they were attacked. Again, like last year, the attacks occurred at different jails but all at the same time. During the press conference, the *Times* took several pictures of us; all the while the *Times* reporter asked us many questions (and received right-to-the-point answers). The next morning, I searched through my copy of the *Times* and found absolutely no mention of our press conference. On the television news that evening, only two (making it at the "top of the hour") broadcast the conference, though there were four television cameras with reporters asking questions. Both were Spanish-speaking stations.

It so happened that a colleague at work shared a copy of the *Times* Valley Edition that included a picture and story. Voice of Citizens Together director Glenn Spenser, who had spearheaded the press conference, was quoted extensively. Why wouldn't the *Times* print this story in its main edition which reaches most black people? After all, we were talking of black inmates being attacked. So much for the "people's right to know!"

CONTI: *What about the schools? Do you think a carelessly liberal slant on race in America is promoted in the classroom?*

FOSTER: I have often said that American public schools have gone from academic learning centers to socialist training camps. It was in the 1960s that I encountered the "psychiatric education movement"—though, certainly, there is evidence of its existence prior to those years. As a first-year teacher, I was required to undergo "training" in Values Clarification. Rogerian education (psychologist Carl Rogers' theory that academic evaluation would "damage" a child's "self-esteem") has worn many hats: Encounter groups, Self-Esteem Training, and its latest banner, Outcome-based Education (OBE). In addition to this psychological assault on the minds of our children, those youngsters in so-called at-risk, impoverished, multicultural schools are given a second whammy: "hate that white-and-racist America" propaganda.

At many schools in the so-called inner cities, one would be hard-pressed even to find an American flag—much less students pledging their allegiance to America. In some of these schools, there is what is called an "African-American flag" (red, green, and black), and students pledge allegiance to Africa—without any idea whatsoever as to which country on the African continent they are pledging their loyalty.

CONTI: *Ezola, what is your assessment of the state of the black family in America today?*

FOSTER: Honestly, Joe, I disdain all-encompassing "state of the black man" or "state of the black family" phrases. Just as in any other race of people, we really are not all alike. I believe that the state of the American family is such that the attacks against its very existence are being met more forcefully. We define the American family as husband and wife (man and woman)—and we believe in love and marriage before baby and carriage. Immorality has left in its wake too many unwed pregnancies, increased teen suicides, crime, corruption, and degradation. But immorality in public places is being challenged. I believe the pendulum is swinging toward a more moral society.

CONTI: *Do you think that black Americans today have more appreciation for America than have past generations of black Americans?*

FOSTER: Those black Americans who were around during World War II and those born prior to the sixties, I believe, are much more patriotic, more appreciative of America. The sixties' political movements were all aimed at America and the institutions that make it a great country: belief in God attacked by the Homosexual Movement, belief in country attacked by the Black Movement.

These movements have had the greatest impact on so-called black communities. These movements have taken their heaviest toll on the hearts and minds especially of young people in so-called black communities.

CONTI: *What would be your prescription for restoring traditional values to*

American society—or do you think that these values are already sufficiently present?

FOSTER: As a family values organization, we subscribe to the four cardinal virtues: justice, prudence, fortitude, temperance. We do not agree with the latest in "Rogerian education" as expressed in Hillary Rodham Clinton's book title, *It Takes a Village to Raise a Child.* Rather, we agree with Mark Thornhill's book title (as reported in the *North County Times*, Sunday, January 21, 1996), "No, It Takes Parents Whose Authority Isn't Undermined by Meddling Government Socialists to Raise a Child."

A prescription, then, for restoring traditional values to American society is that government—from the highest to the local level—ought to give American public schools, by legislation, the task of teaching our children the true meaning of America as "one nation under God." That would be teaching children their American heritage, not at all "establishing a religion"—as the rhetoric goes.

Furthermore, to strengthen the American family, we need a government that would look at all legislation now in effect that undermines the spiritual and legal meaning of the family, that usurps the authority of parents over their children, that provides for psychiatry and psychology in public education programs—and immediately repeal them all.

CONTI: *What do you think is the degree of white racism in this country? Is it increasing or decreasing?*

FOSTER: Gee, how do we really know that someone is mistreating us because of racism or stupidity? Whenever a negative incident occurs between people of different races, one or the other can easily attribute the act to racism. People who believe racism is lurking around every corner will walk into it.

NOTE

Held January 24, 1996, in Los Angeles.

25

"THE SAGE OF SOUTH CENTRAL":
AN INTERVIEW WITH LARRY ELDER

Brad Stetson

STETSON: *Larry, you have an impressive background.[1] You hold a political science degree from Brown University and a law degree from the University of
Michigan. You practiced law for several years and hosted your own television
show in Cleveland. Now, since 1994, you've been hosting your own talk radio
show here in Southern California. What is it about this work that you most
enjoy, and what do you find most challenging about it?*

ELDER: What I enjoy the most is having the potential to alter the way people
think. I don't have any illusions about changing a liberal into a card-carrying
conservative, but I do think I have the ability sometimes to suggest to people
that perhaps they ought to look at the world differently. The hardest part of
my work, of course, is making the show fresh and lively every day.

S: *When I hear your show, I'm struck by how often you are attacked by callers,
especially by black callers who disagree with your views about race and racial
politics. How do you stay enthusiastic and upbeat about your work when, every
day, for four hours, you have to fend off what are often some very vitriolic callers?*

ELDER: I feel that if I were not being attacked, that would be a sign that I
am not speaking the truth. Like anybody, I have a heart, and a soul, and I'm
sensitive, so I would be lying if I said it didn't bother me. But it would bother
me more if the price of not being attacked was to be untrue. That would

definitely bother me more. But I also have the benefit of feeling that the attacking callers are wrong, flat-out dead wrong. It's one thing to be attacked by someone with a defensible point of view. As you know, I take a lot of tough positions. I am in favor of the death penalty. But I also think there is a very disciplined argument that it is immoral. I am in favor of the legalization of drugs, but there is a defensible argument that this is not an appropriate position to take. So it's one thing to be criticized on these issues. But to be attacked because I think that racism is not public enemy number one, to me that is a badge of honor because it shows I am saying something that is true, and offends people because they wish to cling to a false notion.

S: When I hear you being attacked on the radio, it reminds me of remarks Glenn Loury has made about the existential predicament of the black conservative or the black dissident in America. On the one hand, when he expresses his views, he is accused by other black people of being a "race betrayer," a sell-out, an Uncle Tom. On the other hand, many white conservatives who wholeheartedly agree with him, misconstrue his message and manifest a certain passivity and indifference to black progress. This inadvertently gives a measure of credence to black liberals' charges that black conservatives are giving aid and comfort to the enemy, that they allow those whites—conservative or not—who truly are racists to feel comfortable in their hostility to black mobility. Do you ever feel that you are caught between a rock and a hard place in this way?

ELDER: Yes, I think any black American who is "conservative" feels that tension. But I would not agree with the idea that many white conservatives have demonstrated a passivity about black progress. Many conservatives feel that one's ability to make or break one's life is in one's own hands, and that certain public policy positions like welfare and high taxes hurt everybody. I don't feel a need for a "white conservative" to have a special fervor for the black plight. If the black plight is in part the result of bad public policies that affect us all, there is no reason why a white conservative should have to have some sort of special empathy for blacks as opposed to Appalachian whites. I expect a true conservative to be concerned about lack of productivity, the damage high taxes do, the damage excessive regulation does, the fact that Head Start and farm subsidies and all sorts of other programs simply don't work and are an affront to our capitalistic system. If Bob Dole or Jack Kemp doesn't go out of his way to say something nice about black people, that doesn't bother me. In fact, I think it would be condescending. I've heard some black conservatives say, "Let's get rid of affirmative action, but what are we going to put in its place?" What does that mean? It's just programmatic thinking, there's got to be some sort of "program," some sort of "solution." The solution is get off your ass and work hard, stop blaming the white man, stop bitching and moaning.

S: So in your view, nonblack Americans need not, indeed ought not, sense any urgency to further black progress because of the American history of racism against black people?

ELDER: No. All a state can be, is just in its own time. A white person's job is the same as a black person's job: be a good, decent, and just human being; kind and caring toward your parents, kind and caring toward your family, and if you are an employer who must stay competitive, your job is to hire the best and the brightest irrespective of race, color, or creed. That is all any of us have an obligation to do or to be.

S: Interesting.

ELDER: What do you think of that?

S: Well, I think it's a strong point, a strong perspective. I've always been of the opinion that socially and politically, the basic moral standard is that individual people should be held responsible for their own individual behavior. This rules out obligations on the part of contemporary white people toward contemporary black people because some white people in the past victimized black people in the past. It seems to me that what you've articulated is simply individualism, as opposed to the totalitarian, collectivist morality that really holds sway today, where people are treated as groups, and not only that, but some groups have unique moral duties to other groups, for example, whites to blacks. This is philosophically very hard to justify. I think the basic question is, "Will our moral universe be based on current realities, or the sins of dead people?"

ELDER: The answer is, in my opinion, current realities. We could outline a scenario in which Jews, for example, should be very vengeful today. Assuming the truth of the biblical story that the Jews were enslaved by the Egyptians, and assuming you accept the Afrocentric notion that Egyptians are black, then perhaps Jews today are owed reparations by blacks? We could go on forever like this. What kind of obligations do we owe Mexicans, since someone might argue that the Mexican-American War was really about stealing Texas and California from them? What about the Chinese workers who came to this country as Coolies? What about the Irish who came here as indentured servants? Everybody has a case; at what point do we say "Let's try to be just today?"

S: That's well said; it really uncovers some of the foundational assumptions of the American Left today. I wanted to ask you, Larry, about the campaign by a disgruntled black "community group" in Los Angeles to take you off the air. They disagree with your views about race and racial politics and therefore want you off the radio. What do you find most frustrating about the whole thing?

ELDER: The lies they tell about me. I read on the air recently a flier of theirs which they had been handing out. The flier said, "Larry Elder believes: blacks are lazy; blacks are unintelligent; blacks are uneducated; blacks are immoral; blacks are *the* cause of crime in America." There were no citations, no quotes, no dates when I allegedly said these things, nothing. Just a listing of what they claimed were my views. But they are all lies.

S: Was this flier signed by anyone?

ELDER: No, but it did have a phone number at the bottom that you could call, as it said, "for more information." Now, these statements on the flier weren't distortions, they weren't fair interpretations of things that I had said—they were *outright lies*. It is most frustrating to encounter this refusal to fairly characterize and criticize my positions. If they did that, it would be fine. But I never even come close to saying blacks are lazy, blacks are immoral, blacks are *the* cause of crime in America; I have not even come close to saying those things. The other thing that is so frustrating is the refusal of these and other critics of mine to come on the air and debate me. I offered a free and open platform for anyone from that organization to come on the air at KABC and tell me what they think of me, but they won't do it. I have called them repeatedly, my producer has called them, but they won't even return our calls.

S: I have not ever seen any white conservatives mount a drive to remove a white liberal from the air. To what do you attribute the drive of black liberals—people of the "civil rights" mindset—to have a black libertarian like you silenced?

ELDER: Before I answer your question, let me just say I'm happy you called me a black libertarian, although I don't describe myself as a Libertarian, with a capital "L." Look at my views. I'm pro-choice. I believe that drugs should be made legal. (By the way, since there are so many black men behind bars because of drug trafficking, it amazes me that black leadership has not taken this position. To the extent we are concerned about all these black men behind bars—and since a large number of them have not committed violent offenses—why aren't Maxine Waters, Jesse Jackson, Mark Ridley-Thomas, and others fighting to change the drug laws?) I've also said that people of the same sex should be allowed to be married, prostitution should be legalized, and gambling should be fully legalized.

But the only issue with which a lot of people—like those behind that flier—are angry at me is the race question. It really boils down to two things:

Is racism the reason for the black plight today, and how much racism remains in America today? Those are the two fundamental topics on which I've angered people. Racism/slavery is not the primary cause of the black plight today, and racism as a factor in black progress in America is almost insignificant. Those two views drive black liberals nuts, and here's the reason: If you have driven your car into a ditch, and you can blame somebody else for this, it isn't so bad. But if your car is in the ditch, and somebody has the audacity to suggest that you put it there, that is unacceptable to you. To someone who is living in a one-room apartment, driving a Yugo, and struggling economically, the ability to blame slavery and racism for these things is psychologically very comforting. But if someone like Larry Elder comes on the air and says, "Get off your ass and make it happen, don't blame the white man, they aren't out to get you, there is no organized conspiracy against blacks, there are individual bigots of course, but they aren't powerful enough to stop you if you are otherwise prepared and willing to work hard—with hope and optimism," this is unacceptable to people. They don't want to hear that. What I and those like me have done is blown people out of the cocoon of victimhood, the warm and secure cocoon of victimhood, and that is scary to people. Freedom is scary.

S: That is a provocative psychological analysis of the commitment to racism.

ELDER: What else could account for people so misstating my views? How can anyone listen to someone like me on a day-to-day basis—even if they disagree with me—and put out a totally false and defamatory flier like that? They don't even do that to Newt Gingrich! It is not rational behavior.

S: It is a form of character assassination. Has any element of mainstream media come to your defense, as I'm sure they would if white conservatives were trying to get a liberal off the air?

ELDER: No.

S: This raises the question of what some social critics, including your colleague Dennis Prager, have called a double morality: one set of rules for nonblacks, one set of rules for blacks.

ELDER: This is clearly true. I was watching C-SPAN a couple days ago. Jesse Jackson was giving a speech commemorating Martin Luther King, Jr.'s, birthday. During the speech he referred to Newt Gingrich as a "present danger," and later on he referred to him as "corrupt." Can you imagine what would have happened if Bob Dole gave a speech in which he called Jesse Jackson a "present danger" and "corrupt"? Suppose Newt Gingrich had said these things about the First Lady, it would have been headline news. William Safire called her a "congenital liar," and people are still talking about that. Is that any different from Jesse Jackson calling Newt Gingrich "corrupt"? Yet nobody challenged Jackson as to a basis for that charge, even though nobody has charged Gingrich with any crimes.

S: What is your analysis of why the mainstream media are so intimidated about criticizing blacks who say those things. Is it just that they don't want to be called "racist"?

ELDER: That is part of the reason. Black anger is, today, as strong as a force of nature. It is a powerful, unpleasant thing to have directed at you. Another reason is that—as hackneyed as this sounds—most reporters are liberals. If you asked them their political affiliation, the vast majority of them would say they are Democrats. They identify with the downtrodden, they pull for the underdog. Now there are exceptions obviously, but look at how the health care debate was covered. Where was the balanced reporting that challenged the assumption of the need for a new health care plan? Where was the balanced reporting of the views of some economists who not only said we did not need a new health care plan, but we already had socialized medicine— Medicare—and that was what was driving the cost of medical care so high? This point of view was not heard.

So, as liberals, a lot of reporters believe that racism remains a tremendous part of American life. In part, this is because reporters are like cops. When I was in college I studied about police work, and I recall one of the books saying cops often have a cynical and jaundiced view about life because, as the book said, "they see life from the rectum." Reporters often see this side of life too. Their job is to report on the sensational, the unpleasant, the ugly, so they see the bigots and what the bigots do, but they don't see the episodes of racial fairness.

For example, just today, someone approached me who recognized me from a television promotional spot my station had been running, and said, "Larry, I want to shake your hand, I love your show." The man went on to say that he owns a pool cleaning company, and that whenever he has to hire anybody, he always tries to hire the best person he can find. Eight years ago, he said, he hired a young black man, who has since become his closest friend. This young man excelled as a pool cleaner, and was so inventive and creative he even invented two new tools to use on the job. The man said that when these tools are marketed they will revolutionize the pool cleaning business. He went on to say that a lot of his clients are in Beverly Hills, and they all gave the young black pool cleaner a double-take when they saw him—even his black clients did this—because they had never seen a black pool cleaner. But the owner said that this young guy does a good job, he has a pleasant attitude, and as a result, everybody loves him.

This is the sort of story reporters don't cover. Nobody ever hears about people like this young black pool cleaner. But if this young man goes to Beverly Hills to clean a pool, rings somebody's doorbell, and the homeowner calls 911 on him, then you'll read about it in the *L.A. Times.* I remember reading a story in the *L.A. Times* recently about how black tradespeople working in predominantly nonblack areas are treated. They interviewed about twenty-five or thirty tradespeople—electricians, plumbers, and so on—who reported instances when they had been walking up someone's driveway and the homeowner called the police, and the police came out and hand-cuffed them. And other similar stories were reported in this article. So after I read the piece I went on the air. I said I don't doubt that these things happened, and I'm not offering explanations for them. But I hope there is a piece in the paper next week about white tradespeople who work in Compton and Watts, and let's find out about the kind of treatment they've been get-ting.

Right now I'm having my house remodeled. The other day a guy came out to work on my roof. He was white. He said he was recently shot at in Compton, while putting on a roof. People *actually* shot at him.

S: That kind of story doesn't make the papers.

ELDER: No, it doesn't. Recently, I was talking on the air about blacks being harassed in predominantly white neighborhoods. I said, let's do an experi-ment. Let's have five black guys, late at night, two o'clock in the morning, just walk through Bel Air, Beverly Hills, or Brentwood, just walk around, and we'll see what happens to them. Let's also take five white guys, and let them walk around Compton or Watts or East L.A. and let's see what happens to them. Let's see whose experience is more unpleasant. Now I don't doubt that the police might pull up and stop the black guys walking around Beverly Hills. But let me tell you something, it won't be the police who stop those white guys in Watts and Compton. A story like this, though, won't be cov-ered. White racism is one thing, black racism is something entirely different.

S: Some commentators have claimed that in this country there has been a rise of late in black racism. While there certainly has not been an annihilation of white racism, white racial attitudes have improved over time, but black racial attitudes have deteriorated, and now black racism in America is a substantial problem. The rise to national prominence of Louis Farrakhan is indicative of that. Do you agree with that perspective?

ELDER: I have a somewhat different perspective from that. I've seen studies that show, for example, a greater degree of anti-Semitism among young blacks than among older blacks. There is a greater degree of anti-white sentiment among younger blacks than among older blacks. However, I am also aware of one survey by a company that tracked the attitudes of 12.5 million American workers, blacks, whites, Hispanics, and Asians. Blacks were asked, "What is your general opinion about progress in America?" and their answers were generally negative. But then when they were asked, "Describe your personal prospects for promotion in your own company," blacks expressed more optimism about their prospects for promotion than did whites. Thirty-two percent of whites, 35 percent of blacks, about 40 percent of Asians, and about 43 percent of Hispanics felt confident about their prospects for promotion. So I think a number of factors are at work here; it's more complicated than a simple rise in black animosity. There is a group-orientation about racism that all of "us" black people must adopt in order to be "down with the brothers." But when black individuals look at their own specific situation, they respond differently. There is a dichotomy between their own real day-to-day personal experiences and what they say is out there in the real world. This is not unlike the dichotomy you see when you ask parents about education in general, and they say public schools are terrible, and then you ask them about their child's school, and they say it is fine, or Congress is doing a bad job, but my congressman's okay.

S: It seems that this reflects the fact that personal relationships often contradict the stereotypical expectations of what members of a given group are all like. I may be suspicious of members of a group, but when I actually form a relationship with someone from that group, I find my suspicions to be unfounded.

ELDER: Yes. I also read something else that I found extremely important. Blacks were asked the following question: "Is past and present discrimination the major reason for the black plight?" Not surprisingly, 85 percent of blacks said yes, and not too surprisingly only 35 percent of whites said yes. This was roughly like the polling data on O.J. Simpson's guilt or innocence: it shows two very different views of America. But this article went on to report the results of asking Hispanics the question, "Is past and present discrimination a major reason for your problems?" Forty-three percent of Hispanics said yes. Blacks were asked, "Is past and present discrimination a major reason for Hispanics' problems?" and 56 percent of them said yes. Thus, a higher percentage of blacks perceived racism against Hispanics than even Hispanics did! The disparity with Asians was even more dramatic. Asians were asked, "Do you think past and present discrimination is a major reason for your problems?" and 20 percent said yes. Blacks were asked, "Do you think past and present discrimination is a major reason for Asians' problems?" and 41 percent said yes, or twice as many blacks perceived racism against Asians than even Asians did! Question: How accurate is our discrimination antenna? How accurate is the judgment of 85 percent of blacks who hold that racism is a major reason for blacks problems?

S: They're either experts at perceiving discrimination or hypersensitive to it.

ELDER: Well, Asians—Chinese and Japanese—on a per-capita basis, make more money than any group in this country, with the exception of Jewish people I believe, so I guess if only these Asians had been more sensitive to the racism against them, they would be even more successful. This is ridiculous!

S: Well, it's indicative of a certain conditioned-ness on the part of a large segment of the black public, to see racism even when it isn't there. In combatting that perspective on the air, do you feel as though you've changed the minds of any of your black listeners?

ELDER: I have in my briefcase here, a tape of a show I did on April 18, 1995. A black man called me up and said, "Larry, I've been listening to you. I used to be homeless, and I would listen to you every day on my Sony Walkman and *I hated you!* I would think 'Who is this guy coming on the radio and telling me that racism is not a major problem?' but I kept listening, and I kept listening, and the more I heard, the more sense you made. After a while I got up off the street and enrolled in drug re-hab, and I am now in a community college. Larry, you are not an Uncle Tom, you inspired me, you motivated me like no one ever has." That was the most moving call I've ever received.

S: That must have been rewarding for you.

ELDER: Of course it was, and I can't answer your question other than to say I know that I changed one person's life. I feel there have got to be more people out there who've been changed.

S: Have you always been a dissident voice on race relations, or did you have a similar type of conversion experience at some point?

ELDER: No, I've always been this way.

S: What accounts for that?

ELDER: I suspect my father. He is a Republican.

S: Doesn't he own a small business?

ELDER: Yes, but before that he was a janitor. He is an illegitimate child, and he doesn't know who his own father is. He was kicked out of his house when he was thirteen by an indifferent mother. After that he held a series of jobs that can only be described as Dickensonian; remember, he's eighty years old and was a teenager during the Depression. He had a rough, rough life. When I was a kid, he worked two jobs as a janitor, cooked for a white family on the weekends, and went to night school four nights a week to get his GED. He did this while raising a family of three sons with a stay-at-home mother. My father has the most incredible, powerful work ethic I have ever, ever seen. And he never blamed the white man for the circumstances of his life. Not once around the dinner table did I hear my father talk about how racist the country was and how white people had done him in.

S: Yet no doubt he experienced virulent racism.

ELDER: Of course he did. He told us all kinds of stories, one, for example, about growing up with the black park and the white park that people would go to on the weekends. The white park was fine, but the black park had chuck holes everywhere, was run-down, and not maintained at all. When my father got out of the military—as a sergeant—after cooking for the soldiers, and he went back to the South to get a job as a short-order cook, nobody would hire him. He came out to Los Angeles because he thought it would be more liberal, but nobody would hire him here either. That's why he became a janitor. If anybody has the right to carry an AK-47, turn his cap backward, and call himself a "blood" or "crip," it's an eighty-year-old black man or woman. But these people don't do that. They say to young people today, "Thank God you have opportunities I didn't have. Thank God the doors are open. Education is free for you, and if you're broke you can still go to a junior college, you can always get a loan from the government to go to college." That is their attitude.

S: So he did not inculcate within you the anger and resentment that is so fashionable today.

ELDER: No, he didn't. I stay in touch with some friends of mine from high school. A close friend of mine, whom I've known since the second grade, changed his name to Abdul Guyidi. He's full of anger and full of rage. I usually don't talk about political things with him, because I don't want to have a big argument with him. But a few years ago I went to see him, and I had just had it. I said to him, "I've known you since the second grade, I know how hard you studied, I know how little you studied. I know how you goofed off, I know how you devoted your life to sports and athletics. I know the decisions you made in your life. *I know you.* You can't tell me that the white man is the reason you are not working right now. You can tell somebody else that, but don't give *me* that."

S: *How did he respond?*

ELDER: Not pleasantly. We yelled and screamed at each other for almost a half-hour. I would like to report that he got his life together and changed, and is working steadily today, but he isn't. But at least he doesn't whine and complain to me anymore. And he defends me against his other friends who hear me on the air and think I'm an Uncle Tom. He has enough courage and self-awareness to know that he put himself where he is today. Our friendship would not have survived if I hadn't been honest with him about how I thought he was viewing the world. I just would not have been able to continue to see him. He would never have been able to lead me to believe that his plight was not his own doing, that he was a victim, because we had the same backgrounds. He and I had exactly the same histories.

S: *What a telling contrast that is. The two of you started at the same place but have ended up in very different circumstances. That says a lot about the value of your perspective. Thank you Larry.*

ELDER: Thank you.

NOTE

Held January 18, 1996, in Los Angeles. Larry Elder hosts "The Larry Elder Show" from 3:00 P.M. to 7:00 P.M. daily on KABC radio in Los Angeles.

1. For further details on Mr. Elder's background, see the interview with him in *Reason* magazine, April 1996, 44–50.

Appendix:

Media and Organizational Resources for the Study of Black Conservatism

---

Americans for Family Values is directed by Ezola Foster. It is a Southern California-based organization that deals with family issues. For more information, write to Americans for Family Values, 2554 Lincoln Boulevard #264, Venice, California, 90291.

The Brotherhood Organization of a New Destiny (BOND) is directed by Jesse Peterson. BOND is a nonprofit self-help organization dedicated to helping young black men grow into maturity. The address is P.O. Box 86253, Los Angeles, California 90086–0253.

Center of the American Experiment, based in Minneapolis, is advised by many prominent conservative leaders and thinkers, including black conservatives such as Roy Innis, Glenn Loury, and Robert L. Woodson. It is a nonpartisan, public policy, and educational institution that brings conservative and alternative ideas to bear on the most difficult issues facing Minnesota and the nation. For more information, write to Center of the American Experiment, 1024 Plymouth Building, 12 South Sixth Street, Minneapolis, Minnesota 55402.

Center for New Black Leadership is a nonprofit, nonpartisan organization that seeks to revive and encourage traditional solutions to social and economic problems in the African-American community. The Center develops and promulgates sound ideas and institutions that are consistent with the black community's long-held commitments to individual initiative and personal responsibility. For more information, contact the Center for New Black Leadership at 733 Fifteenth Street, NW, Suite 700, Washington, D.C. 20005.

The Chicago Independent Bulletin is published by Hurley Green, Sr. It is the most important black weekly newspaper in the country. Articles by Stan Faryna, Thomas Sowell, Armstrong Williams, and Walter Williams are frequently featured here. *The Chicago Independent Bulletin* is published weekly for $15.00 per year. To inquire about subscriptions, write to 2037 W 95th Street, Chicago, Illinois 60643.

Coalition on Urban Affairs is directed by Star Parker. It is a public policy analysis organization that publishes a monthly newsletter. The address for the Coalition on Urban Affairs is 6033 W Century Boulevard, Suite 300, Los Angeles, California 90045.

The David Institute is a Southern California-based research group that is dedicated to the defense of human dignity. The David Institute is strongly supportive of black conservative politics. For information, write to The David Institute, P.O. Box 1248, Tustin, California 92781.

Destiny magazine is edited and published by Emanuel McLittle. It is a fearless, important, and insightful bimonthly publication featuring comprehensive social criticism and political commentary from the perspective of black conservatives. *Destiny* magazine is available from P.O. Box 1000, Selma, Oregon 97538.

Headway magazine (formerly *National Minority Politics*) is published by Willie and Gwen Richardson. This monthly magazine is the premier publication of black and Hispanic conservative thought. Articles appearing in *Headway* are often written by prominent and important black and white conservatives. Subscription information about *Headway* is available from 13555 Bammel N Houston Road, Suite 227, Houston, Texas 77066.

Imprimis is published by Hillsdale College in Hillsdale, Michigan. It records the remarks of prominent thinkers at Hillsdale College's Shavano Institute for National Leadership Seminars. *Imprimis* is a small but impressive publication that periodically features black conservative writers. For more information, write to Hillsdale College, External Affairs, 33 E College Street, Hillsdale, Michigan 49242–9986.

Issues and Views is edited by Elizabeth Wright, and is an indispensable forum for black conservative thought and social criticism. This excellent publication frequently highlights the history of self-sufficiency in American black life. Published quarterly, it is available from Elizabeth Wright, P.O. Box 467, New York, New York 10025.

The Lincoln Review is edited by J.A. Parker. It is an important and venerable journal of black conservative analysis, published by the Lincoln Institute. The Lincoln Institute's address is 1001 Connecticut Avenue NW, Suite 1135, Washington, D.C. 20036.

The National Center for Neighborhood Enterprise (NCNE) is directed by Robert Woodson, Sr. It is a nonprofit organization operating many programs helping lower income black Americans achieve self-sufficiency and financial independence. For more information, write to the National Center for Neighborhood Enterprise at 1367 Connecticut Avenue, NW, Washington, D.C. 20036.

The National Center for Public Policy Research (NCPPR) is directed by NCPPR president Amy Moritz. It is a nonprofit research organization that administers Project 21, a black leadership organization. Project 21 is an extremely valuable networking group that publicizes the views of black conservatives. Information about Project 21 is available from Project 21 at 300 Eye Street, NE, Suite 3, Washington, D.C. 20002.

The New Coalition for Economic and Social Change (NCESC) is directed by Lee Walker. It is a creative and innovative educational black think tank based in Chicago. For information about the New Coalition for Economic and Social Change, write to 300 S Wacker Drive, Suite 601, Chicago, Illinois 60606 or call (312) 427–1290.

Urban Family magazine is edited by Spencer Perkins. It is a strong voice for family-centered black advocacy, and features the efforts and thought of the Christian Community Development Association. *Urban Family* magazine is available from 1909 Robinson Street, Jackson, Mississippi 39209.

SELECTED BIBLIOGRAPHY

This bibliography lists books central to the discussions in this book. It also presents recent sources from many other points of view that are important for consideration of the myriad moral, social, and political issues engaged by black conservative thought.

Abernathy, Ralph. *And the Walls Came Tumbling Down.* New York: Harper and Row, 1989.

Agronsky, Jonathan. *Marion Barry: The Politics of Race.* Latham, N.Y.: British American Publishing, 1991.

America, Richard F., ed. *The Wealth of Races: The Present Benefits of Past Injustices.* Westport, Conn.: Greenwood Press, 1990.

Asante, Molef Kente. *The Afrocentric Idea.* Philadelphia: Temple University Press, 1987.

Baird, Robert M., and Stewart E. Rosenbaum, eds. *Bigotry, Prejudice and Hatred.* Buffalo, N.Y.: Prometheus Books, 1992.

Bartley, Robert L. *The Seven Fat Years: And How to Do It Again.* New York: Free Press, 1992.

Bell, Derrick. *Faces at the Bottom of the Well: The Permanence of Racism in America.* New York: Basic Books, 1992.

Belton, Don, ed. *Speak My Name: Black Men on Masculinity and the American Dream.* Boston: Beacon Press, 1995.

Bennett, Lerone, Jr. *What Manner of Man.* Chicago: Johnson, 1964.

Bennett, William J. *The De-Valuing of America.* New York: Summit Books, 1992.

———. *The Index of Leading Cultural Indicators: Facts and Figures on the State of American Society.* New York: Simon and Schuster, 1994.

Berger, Peter. *Capitalist Revolution, 50 Propositions about Prosperity.* New York: Basic Books, 1986.

———, and Richard John Neuhaus. *To Empower People.* Washington, D.C.: American Enterprise Institute, 1977.

Blankenhorn, David. *Fatherless America: Confronting Our Most Urgent Social Problem.* New York: Basic Books, 1995.

Bloom, Allan. *The Closing of the American Mind.* New York: Simon and Schuster, 1987.

Bolick, Clint. *Changing Course.* New Brunswick, N.J.: Transaction Books, 1988.

———. *In Whose Name?* Washington, D.C.: Capital Research Center, 1988.

———. *The Affirmative Action Fraud.* Washington, D.C.: Cato Institute, 1996.

Bork, Robert H. *Slouching towards Gomorrah: Modern Liberalism and American Decline.* New York: HarperCollins, 1996.

Boxill, Bernard. *Blacks and Social Justice.* Lanham, Md.: Rowman and Littlefield, 1992.

Branch, Taylor. *Parting the Waters: America During the King Years 1954–63.* New York: Simon and Schuster, 1988.

Brimelow, Peter. *Alien Nation: Commonsense about America's Immigration Disaster.* New York: Random House, 1995.

Brown, Tony. *Black Lies, White Lies: The Truth According to Tony Brown.* New York: William Morrow, 1995.

Butler, John Sibley. *Entrepreneurship and Self-Help among Black Americans: A Reconsideration of Race and Economics.* Albany, N.Y.: State University of New York Press, 1991.

Butler, Stuart M., and Anna Kondratas. *Out of the Poverty Trap: A Conservatve Strategy for Welfare Reform.* New York: Free Press, 1987.

Carter, Stephen. *Reflections of an Affirmative Action Baby.* New York: Basic Books, 1991.

Chideya, Farai. *Don't Believe the Hype: Fighting Cultural Misinformation about African Americans.* New York: Penguin Books, 1995.

Collier, Peter, and David Horowitz, eds. *Second Thoughts: Former Radicals Look Back at the Sixties.* Lanham, Md.: Madison Books, 1989.

———, eds. *Second Thoughts about Race in America.* Lanham, Md.: Madison Books, 1991.

Cone, James H. *Black Theology and Black Power.* New York: Seabury Press, 1969.

Conti, Joseph G., and Brad Stetson. *Challenging the Civil Rights Establishment: Profiles of a New Black Vanguard.* Westport, Conn.: Praeger, 1993.

Cose, Ellis. *The Rage of a Privileged Class.* New York: HarperCollins, 1993.

Crouch, Stanley. *Notes from a Hanging Judge.* New York: Oxford University Press, 1990.

———. *The All-American Skin Game.* New York: Random House, 1995.

Cruse, Harold. *Plural but Equal.* New York: William Morrow, 1987.

Darden, Christopher, with Jess Walter. *In Contempt.* New York: HarperCollins, 1996.

Dash, Leon. *When Children Want Children.* New York: William Morrow, 1989.

———. *Rosa Lee.* New York: Basic Books, 1996.

Demuth, Christopher, and William Kristol. *The Neoconservative Imagination: Essays in Honor of Irving Kristol.* Washington, D.C.: American Enterprise Institute, 1995.

Denton, James, ed. *Welfare Reform: Consensus or Conflict.* Lanham, Md.: University Press of America, 1988.

Detlefsen, Robert. *Civil Rights under Reagan.* San Francisco: Institute for Contemporary Studies Press, 1991.

Dittmer, John. *Local People: The Struggle for Civil Rights in Mississippi.* Chicago: University of Illinois Press, 1995.

D'Souza, Dinesh. *Illiberal Education.* New York: Free Press, 1991.

———. *The End of Racism.* New York: Free Press, 1995.

Dyson, Michael Eric. *Reflecting Black: African American Social Criticism.* Minneapolis: University of Minnesota Press, 1993.

Early, Gerald, ed. *Lure and Loathing: Essays on Race, Identity and the Ambivalence of Assimilation.* New York: Penguin, 1993.

Eastland, Terry. *Ending Affirmative Action: The Case for Colorblind Justice.* New York: Basic Books, 1996.

Efron, Edith. *The News Twisters.* Los Angeles: Nash, 1971.

Elliot, Jeffrey M., ed. *Black Voices in American Politics.* San Diego: Harcourt Brace Jovanovich, 1986.

Findlay, James F., Jr. *Church People in the Struggle: The National Council of Churches and the Black Freedom Movement.* New York: Oxford University Press, 1993.

Foster, Ezola. *What's Right for All Americans!* Foreword by Walter Williams. Waco, Tex.: WRS, 1995.

Franks, Gary. *Searching for the Promised Land: An African-American's Optimistic Odyssey.* New York: HarperCollins, 1996.

Fraser, George. *Success Runs in Our Race.* New York: Avon Books, 1994.

Frazier, E. Franklin. *Black Bourgeoisie: The Rise of a New Middle Class.* New York: Free Press, 1957.

Genovese, Eugene. *Roll Jordan Roll: The World the Slaves Made.* New York: Vintage Books, 1972.

Gibbs, Jewell Taylor, ed. *Young, Black and Male in America: An Endangered Species.* Dover, Mass.: Auburn House, 1988.

Gilder, George. *Wealth and Poverty.* New York: Basic Books, 1981.

———. *Visible Man.* San Francisco: ICS Press reissued version, 1995.

Glazer, Nathan. *Affirmative Discrimination: Ethnic Inequality and Public Policy.* New York: Basic Books, 1975.

Green, Shelly, and Paul Pryde. *Black Entrepreneurship in America.* New Brunswick, N.J.: Transaction, 1989.

Greenberg, Jack. *Crusaders in the Courts.* New York: Basic Books, 1994.

Gross, Barry R., ed. *Reverse Discrimination.* Buffalo, N.Y.: Prometheus Books, 1977.

Gutman, Herbert. *The Black Family in Slavery and Freedom 1750–1925.* New York: Vintage Books, 1977.

Hacker, Andrew. *Two Nations: Black and White, Separate, Hostile, Unequal.* New York: Scribner's, 1992.

Harbison, Frederick H. *Human Resources as the Wealth of Nations.* New York: Oxford University Press, 1973.

Harding, Vincent. *There Is a River: The Black Struggle for Freedom in America.* New York: Harcourt Brace Jovanovich, 1991.

Harrison, Lawrence. *Who Prospers? How Cultural Values Shape Economic and Political Success.* New York: Basic Books, 1992.

Haskins, Ethelbert. *The Crisis in Afro-American Leadership.* Buffalo, N.Y.: Prometheus Books, 1988.

Henry, William A., III. *In Defense of Elitism.* New York: Doubleday, 1994.

Herrnstein, Richard J., and Charles Murray. *The Bell Curve: Intelligence and Class Structure in American Life.* New York: Free Press, 1994.

Himmelfarb, Gertrude. *The De-Moralization of Society.* New York: Alfred A. Knopf, 1995.

Hochschild, Jennifer L. *Facing Up to the American Dream: Race, Class, and the Soul of the Nation.* Princeton, N.J.: Princeton University Press, 1995.

Hund, James. *Black Entrepreneurship.* Belmont, Calif.: Wadsworth, 1970.

Hutchinson, Earl Ofari. *Beyond O. J.: Race, Sex and Class Lessons for America.* Los Angeles: Middle Passage Press, 1996.

Ice T. *The Ice Opinion: Who Gives a Fuck?* New York: St. Martin's Press, 1994.

Institute for Contemporary Studies. *The Fairmont Papers.* San Francisco: ICS Press, 1980.

Jaynes, Gerald David, and Robin Williams. *A Common Destiny: Blacks and American Society.* Washington, D.C.: National Academy Press, 1989.

Jencks, Christopher. *Rethinking Social Policy: Race, Poverty and the Underclass.* Cambridge, Mass.: Harvard University Press, 1992.

Jencks, Christopher, and Paul E. Peterson, eds. *The Urban Underclass.* Washington, D.C.: Brookings Institution, 1991.

Jones, James Earl, and Penelope Niven. *James Earl Jones: Voices and Silences.* New York: Charles Scribner's Sons, 1993.

Keyes, Alan. *Masters of the Dream: The Strength and Betrayal of Black America.* New York: William Morrow, 1995.

Kimball, Robert. *Tenured Radicals: How Politics Has Corrupted Our Higher Education.* New York: Harper and Row, 1990.

King, Martin Luther, Jr. *Stride Towards Freedom: The Montgomery Story.* New York: Harper and Row, 1958.

—————. *Strength to Love.* New York: Harper and Row, 1963.

—————. *Why We Can't Wait.* New York: Harper and Row, 1963.

—————. *The Trumpet of Conscience.* New York: Harper and Row, 1967.

—————. *Where Do We Go from Here: Chaos or Community?* New York: Harper and Row, 1967.

Kovel, Joel. *White Racism: A Psychohistory.* New York: Columbia University Press, 1994.

Kozol, Jonathan. *Savage Inequalities.* New York: Crown, 1991.

—————. *Amazing Grace: The Lives of Children and the Conscience of a Nation.* New York: Crown, 1995.

Lawson, Steven F. *In Pursuit of Power: Southern Blacks & Electoral Politics, 1965–1982.* New York: Columbia University Press, 1985.

Lefkowitz, Mary. *Not out of Africa: How Afrocentrism Became an Excuse to Teach Myth as History.* New York: Basic Books, 1996.

Lemann, Nicholas. *The Promised Land.* New York: Alfred A. Knopf, 1991.

Lester, Julius. *Falling Pieces of the Broken Sky.* New York: Little, Brown, 1990.

Levine, Lawrence. *Black Culture and Black Consciousness: Afro-American Thought from Slavery to Freedom.* New York: Oxford University Press, 1978.

Loury, Glenn. *One by One from the Inside Out: Essays and Reviews on Race and Responsibility in America.* New York: Free Press, 1995.

Lynch, Frederick R. *Invisible Victims: White Males and the Crisis of Affirmative Action.* New York: Praeger, 1991.

—————. *The Diversity Machine: The Drive to Change the "White Male Workplace."* New York: Free Press, 1997.

Magnet, Myron. *The Dream and the Nightmare: The Sixties' Legacy to the Underclass.* New York: William Morrow, 1993.

Majors, Richard, and Janet Mancini Billson. *Cool Pose: The Dilemmas of Black Manhood in America.* New York: Simon and Schuster, 1992.

Marable, Manning. *Beyond Black and Right: Rethinking Race in American Politics and Society.* London: Verso, 1994.

Matusow, Alan. *The Unravelling of America.* New York: Harper and Row, 1984.

Mead, Lawrence. *Beyond Entitlement.* New York: Macmillan Press, 1986.

—————. *The New Politics of Poverty.* New York: Basic Books, 1992.

Moses, Wilson Jeremiah. *Black Messiahs and Uncle Toms: Social and Literary Manipulations of a Religious Myth.* University Park: Pennsylvania State University Press, 1993.

Murray, Charles. *Losing Ground.* New York: Basic Books, 1984.

—————. *In Pursuit of Happiness and Good Government.* ICS Press edition. San Francisco: ICS Press, 1994.

Novak, Michael. *The Spirit of Democratic Capitalism.* New York: Simon and Schuster, 1983.

—————. *Free Persons and the Common Good.* Lanham, Md.: Madison Books, 1989.

———, ed. *Democracy and Mediating Structures: A Theological Inquiry.* Washington, D.C.: American Enterprise Institute Press, 1980.

Oliver, Melvin, and Thomas M. Shapiro. *Black Wealth/White Wealth.* New York: Routledge, 1995.

Oliver, William. *The Violent Social World of Black Men.* New York: Lexington Books, 1994.

Patterson, James, and Peter Kim. *The Day America Told the Truth.* New York: Prentice Hall, 1991.

Patterson, Orlando. *Ethnic Chauvinism.* New York: Stein and Day, 1977.

Peake, Thomas R. *Keeping the Dream Alive: A History of the Southern Christian Leadership Conference from King to the Nineteen-Eighties.* New York: Peter Lang, 1987.

Perkins, John M. *Let Justice Roll Down.* Ventura, Calif.: Regal Books, 1976.

———. *With Justice for All.* Ventura, Calif.: Regal Books, 1982.

———. *Beyond Charity: The Call to Christian Community Development.* Grand Rapids, Mich.: Baker Books, 1993.

Pinkney, Alphonso. *The Myth of Black Progress.* Cambridge: Cambridge University Press, 1984.

Pohlman, Marcus D. *Black Politics in Conservative America.* New York: Longman, 1990.

Powell, Colin, with Joseph Persico. *My American Journey.* New York: Random House, 1995.

Prager, Dennis. *Think a Second Time.* New York: HarperCollins, 1995.

Raspberry, William. *Looking Backward at Us.* Jackson: University Press of Mississippi, 1991.

Rector, Robert. *Strategies for Welfare Reform.* Washington, D.C.: Heritage Foundation, 1992.

Rees, Mathew. *From the Deck to the Sea: Blacks and the Republican Party.* Wakefield, N.H.: Longwood Academic, 1991.

Roberts, Paul Craig, and Lawrence M. Stratton. *The New Color Line: How Quotas and Privilege Destroy Democracy.* Washington, D.C.: Regnery, 1995.

Rossum, Ralph. *Reverse Discrimination: The Constitutional Debate.* Chicago: Marcel Dekker, 1980.

Roth, Byron. *Prescription of Failure: Race Relations in the Age of Social Science.* New Brunswick, N.J.: Transaction, 1994.

Ryan, William. *Blaming the Victim.* New York: Vintage Books, 1976.

Sachar, Emily. *Shut up and Let the Lady Teach!* New York: Simon and Schuster, 1991.

Sandel, Michael. *Liberalism and the Limits of Justice.* Cambridge: Cambridge University Press, 1982.

Schlesinger, Arthur M., Jr. *The Disuniting of America: Reflections on a Multicultural Society.* New York: W. W. Norton, 1991.

Schuyler, George S. *Black and Conservative: The Autobiography of George S. Schuyler.* New Rochelle, N.Y.: Arlington House, 1966.

Sigelman, Lee, and Susan Welch. *Black Americans' Views of Racial Inequality.* Cambridge: Cambridge University Press, 1991.

Sleeper, Jim. *The Closest of Strangers.* New York: W. W. Norton, 1990.

Smith, Errol. *37 Things Every Black Man Needs to Know.* Valencia, Calif.: St. Clair Rene, 1991.

————. *37 More Things Every Black Man and Woman Needs to Know.* Valencia, Calif.: St. Clair Rene, 1994.

————, and Matt Ember. *101 Reasons Not to Be a Liberal.* Valencia, Calif.: St. Claire Rene, 1994.

Smith, James, and Finis Welsch. *Closing the Gap: Forty Years of Economic Progress for Blacks.* Santa Monica, Calif.: Rand Corporation, 1986.

Sniderman, Paul M., and Thomas Piazza. *The Scar of Race.* Cambridge, Mass.: Harvard University Press, 1993.

Sobel, Lester A. *Quotas and Affirmative Action.* New York: Facts on File, 1980.

Sowell, Thomas. *Race and Economics.* New York: Longman, 1975.

————. *Ethnic America.* New York: Basic Books, 1981.

————. *Knowledge and Decisions.* New York: Basic Books, 1981.

————. *Pink and Brown People.* Stanford, Calif.: Hoover Institution Press, 1981.

————. *The Economics and Politics of Race.* New York: William Morrow, 1983.

————. *Civil Rights: Rhetoric or Reality?* New York: William Morrow, 1984.

————. *Compassion Versus Guilt.* New York: William Morrow, 1987.

————. *A Conflict of Visions.* New York: William Morrow, 1987.

————. *Preferential Policies.* New York: William Morrow, 1990.

————. *Inside American Education.* New York: Free Press, 1992.

————. *Race and Culture: A Worldview.* New York: Basic Books, 1994.

————. *The Vision of the Annointed: Self Congratulation as a Basis for Social Policy.* New York: Basic Books, 1995.

Staples, Brent. *Parallel Time Growing up Black and White.* New York: Pantheon Books, 1994.

Steele, Shelby. *The Content of Our Character: A New Vision of Race in America.* New York: St. Martin's Press, 1990.

————. *The End of Oppression.* New York: HarperCollins, 1996.

Sykes, Charles L. *A Nation of Victims.* New York: St. Martin's Press, 1992.

Taulbert, Clifton L. *When We Were Colored.* New York: Penguin Books, 1989.

Taylor, Jared. *Paved with Good Intentions.* New York: Carrol and Graf, 1992.

Teague, Bob. *The Flip Side of Soul.* New York: William Morrow, 1989.

Thomas, Clarence. *Confronting the Future.* Washington, D.C.: Regnery-Gateway, 1992.

Thornbrough, E. L., ed. *Booker T. Washington.* Englewood Cliffs, N.J.: Prentice-Hall, 1969.

Webster, Yehudi O. *The Racialization of America.* New York: William Morrow, 1992.

West, Cornel. *Keeping Faith: Philosophy and Race in America.* New York: Routledge, 1993.

———. *Race Matters.* Boston: Beacon Press, 1993.

Wideman, John Edgar. *Fatheralong: A Meditation on Fathers and Sons, Race and Society.* New York: Pantheon Books, 1994.

Wilbanks, William. *The Myth of a Racist Criminal Justice System.* Monterey, Calif.: Brooks/Cole, 1987.

Williams, Armstrong. *Beyond Blame: How We Can Succeed by Breaking the Dependency Barrier.* New York: Free Press, 1995.

Williams, Constance. *Black Teenage Mothers: Pregnancy and Child Rearing from Their Perspective.* Lexington, Mass.: Lexington Books, 1991.

Williams, Patricia. *The Alchemy of Race and Rights.* Cambridge, Mass.: Harvard University Press, 1991.

Williams, Walter. *The State Against Blacks.* New York: McGraw-Hill, 1982.

———. *All It Takes Is Guts.* Washington, D.C.: Regnery-Gateway, 1987.

———. *Do the Right Thing.* Stanford, Calif.: Hoover Institution Press, 1995.

Wilson, James Q., and Glenn C. Loury. *From Children to Citizens,* Vol. 3. New York: Springer-Verlag, 1987.

Wilson, William Julius. *The Truly Disadvantaged.* Chicago: University of Chicago Press, 1978.

———. *When Work Disappears.* New York: Alfred A. Knopf, 1996.

———. *The Declining Significance of Race.* Chicago: University Chicago Press, 1980.

Woodson, Robert L. *Black Perspectives on Crime and the Criminal Justice System.* Boston: G. K. Hall, 1977.

———. *A Summons to Life.* Cambridge, Mass.: Ballinger, 1981.

———. *Youth Crime and Urban Policy.* Washington, D.C.: American Enterprise Institute, 1981.

———. *On the Road to Economic Freedom.* Washington, D.C.: Regnery-Gateway, 1987.

Wortham, Anne. *The Other Side of Racism.* Columbus: Ohio State University Press, 1981.

———. *Restoring Traditional Values in Higher Education: More Than Afrocentricism.* Washington, D.C.: The Heritage Lectures no. 316.

Zelnick, Bob. *Backfire: A Reporter's Look at Affirmative Action.* Washington, D.C.: Regnery-Gateway, 1996.

INDEX

ABOUT THE EDITORS AND CONTRIBUTORS

MAZHAR ALI AWAN holds a B.S. in Economics from George Mason University. He is currently an international and development economic consultant. As a computer systems consultant, Mr. Awan has worked for Robertshaw/Siebe Controls Inc., the Mobil Corporation, and Maxima Business Systems, among others.

KATHLEEN M. BRAVO was born in Jamaica, and is a writer and an accountant now living in New Jersey. She frequently comments on political issues and is a member of the Advisory Board for Project 21 in Washington, D.C.

JOSEPH E. BROADUS earned his J.D. from Florida State University and is currently teaching law at George Mason University's School of law, where he has taught both constitutional and employment discrimination law. He is a member of the Virginia Council on Equal Employment Opportunity, and is a former law clerk to Judge Joseph W. Hatchett. Prior to joining the law faculty, he was counsel to the Florida House of Representatives Committee on Retirement Personnel and Collective Bargaining.

JOSEPH H. BROWN is a graduate of the University of Iowa. He is an editorial writer with the *Tampa Tribune*. He is also a columnist for *Headway* and has had articles published in *Destiny* magazine, *Chronicles*, and the *Chicago Trib-*

une. Mr. Brown has served as the editorial page editor for the *Iowa City Press-Citizen* and was a columnist with the *Des Moines Register.*

DIANN ELLEN CAMERON is a professional social worker in New York City where she directs and manages a foster care and pre-adoption division at a private child welfare agency. She also practices family mediation and chairs a local task force on Criminal and Juvenile Justice. A former Everett Scholar and recipient of many professional awards, Ms. Cameron lives in the Bronx, where she divides her time between her family and completing her second novel.

JOSEPH G. CONTI holds a Ph.D. in Social Ethics from the University of Southern California. He is co-author of *Challenging the Civil Rights Establishment* (Praeger, 1993) and has published in *Social Justice Review, Intercollegiate Review, Philanthropy, Culture and Society, Destiny* magazine, and other periodicals. He is a research associate at The David Institute and a lecturer in Philosophy at Kansas City Kansas Community College.

STEVEN CRAFT is a graduate of Harvard University's School of Divinity. He is also preparing for ordination as a Baptist minister and has worked with Prison Fellowship in helping prison inmates recover their lives. Mr. Craft is a National Advisory Committee member of Project 21, and has spoken on several radio and television programs across the country for Project 21.

STUART DEVEAUX is a graduate of Howard University in Washington, D.C. His editorials have appeared in African-American newspapers across the country such as the *Chicago Independent Bulletin,* the *Louisiana Weekly, Afro-Times,* and the *Dallas Weekly.* Mr. DeVeaux has also served in the outreach office of Empower America, a conservative public policy organization.

LARRY ELDER earned a Bachelor of Science degree in Political Science from Brown University and a J.D. degree from the University of Michigan. For several years, he practiced law, owned his own attorney-search firm, and hosted a political affairs program on public television in Cleveland. Currently, he has his own afternoon talk show on KABC radio in Los Angeles. He has hosted shows on CNBC cable television and published social commentary in the *Los Angeles Daily News,* as well as other periodicals.

STAN FARYNA holds a B.A. degree in Interdisciplinary Studies from the University of Southern California, and is a graduate student at the Catholic University of America's School of Philosophy. Mr. Faryna is currently Director of Research for the Chicago-based think tank, New Coalition for Economic and Social Change. He also serves as a Research Associate for The

David Institute and is nationally syndicated columnist with USA Features. He has served as director of Project 21 and as a research and editorial assistant for 1993 Templeton prize-winner and theologian Michael Novak.

EZOLA FOSTER holds a B.S. degree in Business from Texas Southern University and a Master's degree in School Management and Administration from Pepperdine University. A great-grandaughter of black Americans who were slaves, Mrs. Foster has worked in the Los Angeles Unified School District for over thirty years. She is a frequent television commentator on political controversies, having appeared on *Larry King Live, Oprah, Newsmaker Saturday,* and other programs. She is the author of the excellent and spirited book, *What's Right for All Americans* with a foreword by Walter Williams (WRS Publishing, 1995). Mrs. Foster is president of Americans for Family Values, 2554 Lincoln Boulevard #264, Venice, California, 90291.

MARIVIC C. FRANCIS holds a B.A. in Psychology from the University of California Los Angeles. She is the personal assistant to Jesse Peterson and director of Public Relations for BOND.

GARY FRANKS, former Congressman for the fifth district of Connecticut, served in the United States House of Representatives from 1990 to 1996. Prior to his election, Congressman Franks worked for three Fortune 500-type companies as a labor relations executive. During his tenure in Congress, Mr. Franks introduced legislative initiatives focusing on the revitalization of urban areas and on welfare reform. He is the author of *Searching for the Promised Land: An African-American's Optimistic Odyssey* (1996).

ROBERT A. GEORGE is presently writer to the Speaker of the United States House of Representatives. In this capacity he has published articles in numerous newspapers and magazines across the country. He previously served as legislative assistant to former Congressman Michael Huffington (R-Calif.) and on the staff of the Republican National Committee's finance division. Mr. George is a graduate of St. John's College in Annapolis, Maryland.

BRIAN W. JONES is a graduate of Georgetown University and the UCLA School of Law. He is president of the Center for New Black Leadership and serves on the National Advisory Board of Project 21. As president of the Center, Mr. Jones has written for *National Minority Politics, Human Events, National Review,* and other periodicals. He has testified before the U.S. Senate Labor and Human Resources and Judiciary Committees on the subject of affirmative action. He is currently on leave of absence from Sheppard, Mullin, Richter & Hampton, a Los Angeles-based law firm.

PETER KIRSANOW is currently labor counsel for Leaseway Transportation Corporation, as well as a partner in the firm Allport, Miller and Kirsanow, and adjunct professor at the Cleveland-Marshall College of Law. Mr. Kirsanow served as chief labor attorney for the city of Cleveland, Ohio, from 1984 to 1990, and has extensive experience in labor law and policy. He has been a frequent critic of federal labor policies that adversely affect the African-American community. His writings on labor policy issues, health care, and welfare reform have been featured in newspapers nationwide.

TELLY LOVELACE is a senior at the University of Maryland in College Park, where he is majoring in Economics. He is a member of the National Advisory Committee of Project 21 and has served as a research assistant at the CATO Institute. Mr. Lovelace served as a research assistant in the House Small Business Subcommittee on Regulation and Paperwork in 1995 and worked on the Bill Brock for U.S. Senate campaign in 1994.

DEROY MURDOCK is a New York writer and president of Loud & Clear Communications, a marketing and media consultancy. He is an adjunct fellow with the Fairfax, Virginia-based Atlas Economic Research Foundation. His political commentary frequently appears in the *Washington Times*, the *Orange County Register*, and numerous other periodicals nationwide. He is an on-air contributor to MSNBC, the new cable and internet service from Microsoft and NBC News. He also has been a featured guest on dozens of radio and television discussion programs in the United States and abroad. Mr. Murdock received a bachelor's degree in Government from Georgetown University and an MBA from New York University.

JESSE PETERSON is a grassroots community activist in Los Angeles. He is the founder and president of the Brotherhood Organization of a New Destiny (BOND), a nonprofit self-help organization dedicated to helping young black men grow into maturity. Mr. Peterson has appeared on *Donahue, Geraldo, Nightline,* and other television shows, as well as numerous radio programs across the country.

GWEN RICHARDSON holds a B.S. in Marketing from Georgetown University. She is editor of *Headway* magazine (formerly *National Minority Politics* magazine). With her husband, Willie Richardson, she has co-authored articles for the *Houston Chronicle*, the *Atlanta Constitution, Emerge, Destiny,* and several other periodicals.

WILLIE RICHARDSON holds a B.S. in Electronics from the University of Houston. He is the publisher of *Headway* magazine, and co-founder and president of Minority Mainstream, a national grassroots membership and lobbying organization dedicated to promoting the values of strong families, individual responsibility, free enterprise, and reduced government.

ERROL SMITH is CEO of Smith Friday enterprises, a marketing and management firm. He is the author of four provocative books on race, politics, and business, and he is currently a columnist for *Headway* magazine. He has published in the *Wall Street Journal*, the *Los Angeles Times, Reason* magazine, and other periodicals. He is the founder of the Leadership Circle, an organization dedicated to teaching young black men entrepreneurial principles and leadership.

SHELBY STEELE wrote *The Content of Our Character* (1990), a number one national bestseller that changed the course of American racial politics. He has written numerous essays for *Harper's*, the *New York Times, Newsweek*, and other national periodicals. Formerly a professor of English at San Jose State University, he is currently a fellow of the Hoover Institution at Stanford University. His latest book is *The End of Oppression* (1996).

BRAD STETSON holds a Ph.D. in Social Ethics from the University of Southern California. He is co-author of *Challenging the Civil Rights Establishment* (Praeger, 1993), author of *Pluralism and Particularity in Religious Belief* (Praeger, 1994), and editor of the anthology *The Silent Subject: Reflections on the Unborn in American Culture* (Praeger, 1996). He is director of The David Institute, a social research group.

CLARENCE THOMAS has a B.A. from Holy Cross College and a J.D. from Yale University. He has served as an associate justice for the United States Supreme Court since 1991. He served as a judge for the U.S. Court of Appeals, Washington, D.C., from 1990 to 1991 and was chairman of the U.S. EEOC from 1982 to 1990. Justice Thomas served as assistant secretary for civil rights in the Department of Education from 1981 to 1982 and was legislative assistant to Senator John C. Danforth from 1979 to 1982.

LEE WALKER is the president and CEO for the New Coalition for Economics and Social Change, whose mission is to encourage the pursuit of alternative public policies that promote economic independence and strengthen the institutions of families, schools, churches, and communities. Mr. Walker is also a columnist for *Crain's Chicago Business*. In 1995, Governor Jim Edgar appointed him to be a member of the Illinois Regulatory Review Commission. Mr. Walker also serves on the board of the Heartland Institute.